DESMOND TUTU

Recent Titles in Greenwood Biographies

George S. Patton: A Biography
David A. Smith

Gloria Steinem: A Biography
Patricia Cronin Marcello

Billy Graham: A Biography
Roger Bruns

Emily Dickinson: A Biography
Connie Ann Kirk

Langston Hughes: A Biography
Laurie F. Leach

Fidel Castro: A Biography
Thomas M. Leonard

Oprah Winfrey: A Biography
Helen S. Garson

Mark Twain: A Biography
Connie Ann Kirk

Jack Kerouac: A Biography
Michael J. Dittman

Mother Teresa: A Biography
Meg Greene

Jane Addams: A Biography
Robin K. Berson

Rachel Carson: A Biography
Arlene R. Quaratiello

DESMOND TUTU

A Biography

Steven D. Gish

GREENWOOD BIOGRAPHIES

GREENWOOD PRESS
WESTPORT, CONNECTICUT · LONDON

Library of Congress Cataloging-in-Publication Data

Gish, Steven, 1963-
  Desmond Tutu : a biography / Steven D. Gish.
    p. cm. — (Greenwood biographies)
  Includes bibliographical references and index.
  ISBN 0–313–32860–9
  1. Tutu, Desmond. 2. Church of the Province of Southern Africa—Bishops—Biogra-
phy. 3. Anglican Communion—South Africa—Bishops—Biography. I. Title. II. Series.
BX5700.6.Z8T8737 2004   2004011313
283'.092—dc22

British Library Cataloguing in Publication Data is available.

Library of Congress Catalog Card Number: 2004011313
ISBN: 0–313–32860–9
ISSN: 1540–4900

First published in 2004

Greenwood Press, 88 Post Road West, Westport, CT 06881
An imprint of Greenwood Publishing Group, Inc.
www.greenwood.com

Printed in the United States of America

The paper used in this book complies with the
Permanent Paper Standard issued by the National
Information Standards Organization (Z39.48–1984).

10 9 8 7 6 5 4 3 2 1

Copyright Acknowledgments

The author and publisher gratefully acknowledge permission to reprint extracts from
the following material.

From *Tutu: Voice of the Voiceless* by Shirley du Boulay, copyright © 1988. Reprinted by
permission of Harold Ober Associates Incorporated and David Higham Associates
Limited.

From *The Rainbow People of God* by Desmond Tutu and John Allen, editor, copyright ©
1994 by Desmond Tutu and John Allen. Used by permission of Doubleday, a division of Random House, Inc. and Lynn C. Franklin Associates, Ltd.

From *No Future without Forgiveness* by Desmond Tutu, copyright © 1999 by Desmond
Tutu. Used by permission of Doubleday, a division of Random House, Inc. British
Commonwealth rights for extracts from *No Future without Forgiveness* by Desmond
Tutu published by Rider. Used by permission of The Random House Group Limited.

To the memory of Rod Vahl—teacher, mentor, friend.

CONTENTS

CONTENTS

Photo essay follows page 56.

SERIES FOREWORD

In response to high school and public library needs, Greenwood developed this distinguished series of full-length biographies specifically for student use. Prepared by field experts and professionals, these engaging biographies are tailored for high school students who need challenging yet accessible biographies. Ideal for secondary school assignments, the length, format, and subject areas are designed to meet educators' requirements and students' interests.

Greenwood offers an extensive selection of biographies spanning all curriculum-related subject areas including social studies, the sciences, literature and the arts, history and politics, as well as popular culture, covering public figures and famous personalities from all time periods and backgrounds, both historic and contemporary, who have made an impact on American and/or world culture. Greenwood biographies were chosen based on comprehensive feedback from librarians and educators. Consideration was given to both curriculum relevance and inherent interest. The result is an intriguing mix of the well known and the unexpected, the saints and sinners from long-ago history and contemporary pop culture. Readers will find a wide array of subject choices from fascinating crime figures like Al Capone to inspiring pioneers like Margaret Mead, from the greatest minds of our time like Stephen Hawking to the most amazing success stories of our day like J. K. Rowling.

While the emphasis is on fact, not glorification, the books are meant to be fun to read. Each volume provides in-depth information about the subject's life from birth through childhood, the teen years, and adulthood. A thorough account relates family background and education, traces personal and professional influences, and explores struggles, accomplishments, and contributions. A timeline highlights the most significant life events against a historical perspective. Bibliographies supplement the reference value of each volume.

INTRODUCTION

On April 27, 1994, 62-year-old Desmond Tutu entered a polling station in Guguletu, South Africa, and voted for the first time in his adult life. Black South Africans had never before been allowed to vote in a democratic, national election. For generations, the country's citizens had been divided by apartheid, a legalized system of racial discrimination that benefited the white minority and severely restricted the black majority. Apartheid had been one of the most notorious systems of racial segregation the world had ever seen. The April 1994 election of Nelson Mandela as South Africa's first black president signaled that apartheid had finally ended.

Desmond Tutu dedicated his life to ending apartheid. Some called him South Africa's Martin Luther King Jr. The son of a schoolteacher and a domestic worker, Tutu was an Anglican priest who rose to become general secretary of the South African Council of Churches and the first black South African archbishop of Cape Town. He had been one of the anti-apartheid movement's most visible and effective leaders. During his many travels, speeches, and sermons, he raised the world's consciousness about apartheid and convinced the world to help end it. He ceaselessly advocated nonviolent change when others resorted to violence. He sought to build bridges and promote dialogue between black and white when others sought confrontation. In recognition of his efforts to end apartheid nonviolently, Tutu was awarded the Nobel Peace Prize in 1984, one of the world's highest honors. His words had stirred a nation—and the world.

Tutu remained faithful to his core beliefs throughout his public life. Foremost among his values was Christian compassion. He believed that Christianity obligated him to defend the poor and the oppressed, wherever they might be. He constantly expressed the hopes and dreams of the downtrodden. Racial equality was another of Tutu's core principles. He sought to build a nation—and a world—in which all people could live together as brothers and sisters, regardless of race, creed, or color. He urged South Africans of all races to protest injustice vigorously but nonviolently. Although Tutu always advocated nonviolence, he was neither timid nor cautious when it came to protesting apartheid.

Despite rising black anger over racial injustice, Tutu refused to hate his oppressors. Whites were never his enemy, only the system of apartheid. A less conciliatory leader could have urged black South Africans to abandon peace and nonviolence and seek revenge—to treat whites as some whites had treated them. Once apartheid finally crumbled, Tutu could have retired. Instead he continued to serve his country by agreeing to head South Africa's Truth and Reconciliation Commission. This commission probed past human rights abuses under apartheid and offered forgiveness to those who confessed their misdeeds. Tutu believed that by chairing the commission, he could help heal the wounds of the past in a still racially divided nation.

Although the causes for which he stood were profoundly serious, Tutu was anything but dour or morose. He became well known for his sparkling wit and effervescent personality. He often punctuated his public remarks with humor to illustrate the nonsense inherent in apartheid. Tutu's mirth proved to be a gentle but effective weapon because it captured the absurdity of apartheid in unforgettable ways.

History will remember Desmond Tutu as a man of many gifts. He captivated audiences worldwide with his charismatic oratory. He managed to be forceful and outspoken without sounding bitter. He recognized the humanity of friend and foe alike and, in so doing, became an icon of reconciliation. During the darkest days of apartheid, he persisted against enormous odds and inspired hope for the future.

Tutu's life has not been a series of inevitable triumphs. There were achievements and setbacks, conflicts and coalitions, and most of all, controversies. He was arrested, harassed, threatened, and at times vilified for his beliefs. But he refused to give up. He repeatedly assured all those who would listen that justice would triumph in the end. His passionate commitment to freedom and justice never wavered. In retirement, he continues to inspire the world.

TIMELINE OF EVENTS IN THE LIFE OF DESMOND TUTU

7 October 1931	Birth of Desmond Tutu in Klerksdorp, South Africa.
1943	Anglican priest Trevor Huddleston arrives in South Africa from England.
1943	Tutu moves to Krugersdorp with family.
1945	Enrolls at Western Native Township High School.
1945	Hospitalized for tuberculosis.
1948	National Party government begins to implement apartheid policy.
1950	Finishes high school and passes Joint Matriculation Board exams.
1951	Begins teacher training at Bantu Normal College in Pretoria.
1953	Earns teacher's diploma from Bantu Normal College.
1954	Begins teaching at Madibane High School (formerly known as Western Native Township High School).
1954	Earns BA from the University of South Africa.
1955	Bantu Education Act implemented, requiring black South African schools to stress vocational training and manual labor.
2 July 1955	Marries Leah Shenxane.
1955	Begins teaching at Munsieville High School, Krugersdorp.

14 April 1956 First child (Trevor) is born.

1958 Leaves teaching; begins training to become a priest at St. Peter's Theological College, Rosettenville, Johannesburg.

21 March 1960 Police open fire on antipass demonstration in Sharpeville, killing at least 69 people (black South Africans were required to carry identity documents known as "passes" with them at all times).

1960 African National Congress (ANC) banned by South African government.

1960 Awarded licentiate of theology from St. Peter's; ordained as a deacon and begins preaching in Benoni.

1961 Ordained as a priest; begins preaching in Thokoza, southeast of Johannesburg.

September 1962 Moves to Britain to begin studies at King's College, University of London.

1963 Fourth and last child, a daughter named Mpho, is born in Britain.

1965 Earns Bachelor of Divinity (honors) from King's College, University of London.

1966 Earns Master's of Theology from King's College, University of London.

1967 Begins teaching at Federal Theological Seminary in Alice, South Africa; also becomes Anglican chaplain at nearby Fort Hare University.

1970 Accepts position as lecturer of theology at the University of Botswana, Lesotho, and Swaziland in Roma, Lesotho.

January 1972 Moves with family to London and becomes associate director of the Theological Education Fund of the World Council of Churches.

1975 Returns to South Africa to become Anglican dean of Johannesburg.

6 May 1976 Writes Prime Minister B. J. Vorster to warn him about rising black anger over apartheid.

16 June 1976 Police fire upon student demonstrators in Soweto; unrest escalates in the weeks and months ahead, claiming the lives of hundreds of black South

	Africans and sparking the country's most serious racial crisis to date.
August 1976	Becomes bishop of Lesotho.
March 1978	Becomes general secretary of the South African Council of Churches.
March 1980	South African government refuses to issue Tutu a passport.
May 1980	Arrested with other clergymen while protesting the arrest of Congregationalist minister John Thorne; held overnight in jail.
November 1981	Prime Minister P. W. Botha establishes Eloff Commission to investigate the South African Council of Churches.
September 1982	Addresses the Triennial Convention of the Episcopal Church in New Orleans.
September 1984	New South African constitution implemented; tricameral (three-chamber) parliament meets for the first time; new period of racial unrest begins.
23 October 1984	Addresses the UN Security Council.
7 December 1984	Meets with U.S. President Ronald Reagan at the White House.
10 December 1984	Awarded Nobel Peace Prize in Oslo, Norway.
3 February 1985	Becomes bishop of Johannesburg.
20 July 1985	Partial state of emergency declared in South Africa.
April 1986	Issues formal call for sanctions to be imposed on South Africa.
12 June 1986	Nationwide state of emergency declared in South Africa.
7 September 1986	Becomes archbishop of Cape Town.
2 October 1986	U.S. Congress overrides President Reagan's veto and passes Comprehensive Anti-Apartheid Act.
September 1987	Elected president of the All-Africa Council of Churches.
29 February 1988	Arrested with other clergymen during procession from St. George's Cathedral in Cape Town to Parliament building.
14 August 1989	P. W. Botha resigns as state president; is succeeded by F. W. de Klerk.

13 September 1989	Along with Rev. Allan Boesak, leads protest march of 30,000 people in Cape Town.
2 February 1990	F. W. de Klerk announces plans to unban anti-apartheid groups, release political prisoners, and begin negotiations for a new South Africa.
11 February 1990	ANC leader Nelson Mandela released after 27 1/2 years in prison.
10 September 1990	Leads church delegation to see de Klerk in Pretoria; clerics express concern that a "third force" is fomenting violence in South Africa.
17 June 1992	Migrant workers attack community in Boipatong, killing 46 residents.
10 April 1993	Assassination of Chris Hani, popular leader in the ANC and the South African Communist Party.
26–29 April 1994	South Africa holds its first democratic elections; Tutu votes for the first time.
10 May 1994	Nelson Mandela inaugurated as South Africa's first black president; Tutu leads a prayer at inauguration ceremony in Pretoria.
August 1994	Publicly criticizes new government's pay raises.
October 1994	*The Rainbow People of God* is published.
December 1995	Appointed chairperson of the Truth and Reconciliation Commission.
16 April 1996	Commission begins hearings in East London, South Africa.
23 June 1996	Retires as archbishop of Cape Town; awarded Order of Meritorious Service by President Mandela.
1 July 1996	Becomes archbishop emeritus.
January 1997	Diagnosed with prostate cancer; begins cancer treatment in South Africa and the United States.
1998	Begins two-year visiting professorship at Candler School of Theology at Emory University, Atlanta.
29 October 1998	Presents first five volumes of truth commission report to President Mandela.
November 1999	*No Future Without Forgiveness* is published.
15 June 2000	Desmond Tutu Peace Centre is publicly launched in New York; center bases itself in Cape Town.
7 October 2001	Celebrates 70th birthday.
January 2002	Begins one-semester visiting professorship at the Episcopal Divinity School, Cambridge, Massachusetts.

January 2003   Begins one-semester visiting professorship at the
                University of North Florida, Jacksonville.
21 March 2003   Presents volumes 6 and 7 of truth commission re-
                port to President Thabo Mbeki in Pretoria.
January 2004   Begins visiting professorship at King's College, Uni-
                versity of London.
March 2004   *God Has a Dream* is published.

Chapter 1

BEGINNINGS

Desmond Tutu has often referred to South Africa as a "rainbow" nation. For centuries it has been home to people of diverse races, creeds, and cultures. Indigenous African societies were the first to settle widely in what is now South Africa. They included groups such as the Zulu, Xhosa, Pedi, Tswana, and Sotho. The first permanent European settlers arrived in 1652, when the Dutch East India Company established a refreshment station for its ships in Cape Town. The original Dutch settlers conquered the local Khoikhoi and San peoples in the southwestern Cape and began to construct a society based on white supremacy. Within a few years of their arrival in Cape Town, the Dutch began to import slaves from Madagascar, Mozambique, Malaysia, and Indonesia. The Dutch soon absorbed French and German settlers into their communities. Relationships between Europeans, Africans, and Asians produced mixed-race offspring who would eventually become known as "Coloureds." British settlers arrived in the early nineteenth century; laborers from India arrived later that century. With so many diverse groups within its borders, South Africa was destined to have a rich, yet turbulent, history.

The British gained control over the Cape colony in 1806 and abolished slavery in 1833. Disenchanted with the new British government, some descendants of the early Dutch settlers moved northeast into the interior to escape British rule. As they did so, they clashed with the more densely populated African societies, including the powerful Zulu kingdom. Competition for land in southern Africa became even more intense after diamonds and gold were discovered in the late nineteenth century. Following these mineral discoveries, the British tightened their grip on the region.

They defeated the Zulus at Rorke's Drift and Ulundi in 1879 after suffering tremendous losses at the battle of Isandlwana. Then the British began to covet territory held by the Dutch descendants, who were sometimes known as Boers (farmers). In the Anglo-Boer War of 1899–1902, the British defeated the Boers after a bitter struggle and incorporated the mineral-rich territories into the British empire. The Union of South Africa was created in 1910, uniting the British colonies of the Cape and Natal with the former Boer republics of the Orange Free State and the South African Republic. The Union's new constitution gave white South Africans self-government within the British empire. Black South Africans hoped that the British government would intervene to defend their rights, but such intervention never materialized.

Whites monopolized political and economic power in the Union. In the years after 1910, the South African government built a legal system based on racial segregation and discrimination. For example, the 1913 Native Land Act restricted African land ownership to 7 percent of South African land. The 1923 Urban Areas Act created segregated townships where Africans could be forced to live if they resided in urban areas. The government considered towns and cities to be the preserve of whites. In the words of one official, blacks would only be allowed to live in separate, segregated parts of urban areas if they met the needs of the white population. In 1926, the government passed the Colour Bar Act, which reserved some skilled jobs in mines for white workers. These and many other discriminatory laws were in place at the time of Desmond Tutu's birth.

When Tutu was born, South Africa was ruled by the government of Prime Minister James Hertzog. Only whites and a few blacks in the Cape province could vote, and Hertzog planned to limit rather than expand black South African political and economic rights in the near future. According to the 1936 census, South Africa had approximately 9.5 million people, of whom 69 percent were African; 21 percent white; 8 percent mixed raced; and 2 percent Indian.[1] In the 1930s, the Great Depression eroded the living standards of almost all South Africans, especially the African majority. Many Africans moved into towns and cities in search of work, where they were often housed in poor conditions. The Depression worsened racial inequality and black poverty in South Africa.

It was into this rather harsh world that Desmond Mpilo Tutu arrived on October 7, 1931. He was born in Klerksdorp, a town in the southwestern Transvaal province, to Zachariah and Aletha Tutu. Desmond was so sickly as a baby that his father feared that he would not survive infancy. After his condition began to stabilize, Desmond's grandmother gave him the

middle name "Mpilo," meaning *life*. Desmond had an older sister named
Sylvia and would eventually have a younger sister, Gloria; a brother died
before Desmond was born. The household in which Desmond grew up reflected South Africa's ethnic diversity. His father, Zachariah, was originally from the eastern Cape and spoke Xhosa; his mother Aletha's first
language was Tswana; and his grandmother spoke Sotho. Desmond
learned all three languages as a boy. His family identified themselves as
Africans or South Africans rather than as members of a specific tribe or
ethnic group and Desmond would do the same throughout his life. At the
time of Desmond's birth, Zachariah was the headmaster of a Methodist
primary school in Klerksdorp. Teaching was a relatively good occupation
for black South Africans at the time, since many urban African men
could only find jobs as unskilled workers in the mines or industry. Aletha,
who only had a primary-school education, earned money doing domestic
work for white families.

Klerksdorp was located in a gold-mining area, but the African residents of the town were far from prosperous. Like most black South
African homes at the time, the Tutus' house had no electricity or indoor
plumbing. Families would use a communal tap in the neighborhood
when they needed water. The Tutus and their neighbors were poor, but
this did not trouble Desmond as a child. He and his playmates entertained themselves with what they could find or make. They played soccer with tennis balls and made model cars out of wire and scrap metal.
According to his childhood friends, Desmond had a mild and noncon-
frontational temperament as a youngster. He was small in stature and had
a good sense of humor. Later, Tutu would joke that he resembled his
mother physically—"she was short and stumpy and had a big nose."[2]
Desmond would take after his mother in other ways as well, especially
her inclination to root for the underdog. Eventually Aletha's warmth and
gentleness earned her the nickname "Komotso" (comforter). Desmond's
father was the strict parent in the family and cared deeply about his children's health and education. On Saturdays he would take Desmond for
rides on his bicycle, and sometimes the two would go fishing together.
Desmond was not particularly fond of fishing, but he enjoyed spending
time with his father. Unfortunately, Zachariah occasionally drank too
much and assaulted Aletha, greatly upsetting his son. Memories of these
incidents still pained Tutu years later.[3]

Zachariah and Aletha always insisted that their children be deferential
in the presence of adults. In the Tutu family—and in black South African
households in general—children were expected to be seen and not heard.
As Desmond later wrote,

I remember we were often warned not even to look at grown-ups as they were involved in some animated conversation. Living in cramped quarters it was practically impossible to be interested in one's books, while people were laughing and joking in the same room. We were told to leave the room when other grown-ups came to visit...and we had to be quick about producing the tea (at any old hour), which the "gods" enjoyed guzzling in enormous quantities.[4]

When Desmond was eight years old, his family moved to Ventersdorp so that Zachariah could assume the headmastership of a new school. Ventersdorp was a small town in the Transvaal province about 40 miles north of Klerksdorp. There, Desmond learned to speak Afrikaans, the language of the Afrikaners, who were the descendants of the early Dutch settlers. Desmond often ventured into Ventersdorp's white neighborhoods to pick up the laundry that his mother washed in her home. During these excursions, he sometimes saw black children sifting through garbage at white schools in search of food. He later learned that the wealthier white pupils received subsidized school lunches, while poor black students did not. One of Desmond's role models in Ventersdorp was Ezekiel Mphahlele, who would become a well-known South African writer. Mphahlele encouraged the township youth, including Desmond, to read. He also urged Desmond to keep physically fit. Not only would Mphahlele take his young friend jogging, he also taught Desmond how to box.

Although Desmond had been baptized into the Methodist Church, his family eventually converted to Anglicanism. They made the switch when Desmond's older sister, Sylvia, enrolled at St. Peter's College, one of the most respected black high schools in South Africa. St. Peter's was run by the Anglican-based Community of the Resurrection in Rosettenville. Tutu admired his first Anglican priest in Ventersdorp, Father Sekgaphane. Desmond would sometimes accompany Father Sekgaphane on trips to outlying parishes in the countryside and serve as an altar boy. After services, Father Sekgaphane would preside over a meal, always making sure that "we lesser mortals" were served before he ate. The priest's humility and kindness greatly impressed young Desmond.[5]

Tutu also appreciated his father's encouragement, especially when it came to reading. When asked by an interviewer what book had the most effect on him as a youngster, Tutu said, "I loved reading Aesop's Fables and then Lamb's Tales from Shakespeare. My father used to try and help me, and I got to loving to read, because he allowed me to read comics, which most people said you shouldn't let your child read because they will spoil him. But that gave me an extraordinary hunger for reading. And I was very fortunate; I had very good teachers."[6]

It was in Ventersdorp that Desmond experienced racial prejudice for the first time. As a youngster, he would often ride a bicycle to a local shop to get his father's newspaper, which he would read too. One day while riding to the shop, Desmond encountered a group of white boys who shouted racial insults at him in Afrikaans. In another incident, Desmond watched in disbelief as a young white girl addressed his father as "boy." "There was nothing much my father could do about it," Tutu later recalled. "And you could see him grow small in your very presence because he was embarrassed this was happening in front of his child."[7] Desmond was also deeply troubled when he witnessed his father being stopped by police officers demanding to see his "pass." South African law required African men to carry these identification booklets with them at all times. The booklets contained the individual's name, photograph, date of birth, residence, and employment information. Africans needed to have government officials stamp their pass books in order to live, work, and travel in certain areas. Passes had to be produced on demand; the penalty for not having a valid pass could be imprisonment or a fine or both. Not surprisingly, the pass laws created great resentment among black South Africans, who considered passes symbols of their inferior status in South African society. Even though he was a respected headmaster, Desmond's father could be harassed by police simply because he was black.

In the early 1940s, the Tutus moved to Roodepoort, a town just west of Johannesburg, where Zachariah started working at another school. Conditions in Roodepoort were particularly bad for black residents. Their neighborhoods not only lacked electricity and running water, but the houses were unusually small and cramped. Desmond was in primary school by this time, and he performed well as a pupil in Roodepoort. His classmates admired both his high intelligence and his soccer-playing ability. He even earned the nickname "Dribbling Whiz" for his skills on the soccer field.[8] While living in Roodepoort, Desmond's mother got a job as a cook at the Ezenzeleni School for the Blind, the first such school for Africans in South Africa. It had been established by an English couple, Reverend Arthur Blaxall and his wife, Florence. Desmond often accompanied his mother to the school and was impressed by the Blaxalls' work on behalf of blind Africans. The example the Blaxalls set convinced Desmond that not all whites were oppressors. Another incident underscored this point in a more personal manner. One day when Desmond was with his mother at the Ezenzeleni School, a tall white man in priestly garb tipped his hat to Mrs. Tutu in greeting. Such a gesture was almost unheard of in the racially stratified society of South Africa. Desmond, who was 11 or 12 at the time, never forgot this rare gesture of courtesy from a white man. The man who greeted Aletha was Trevor Huddleston, an Anglican priest based in the Johannesburg neighborhood of Sophiatown. Although he did not know it at the time, Desmond had just glimpsed the man who would become his greatest role model.[9]

NOTES

1. Ellen Hellmann, ed., *Handbook on Race Relations in South Africa* (Cape Town: Oxford University Press, 1949), pp. 6, 9.

2. Desmond Tutu, "Great Conversations" (lecture, University of Minnesota–Twin Cities, 25 February 2003), www.news.mpr.org/programs/midday/listings/md20030303.shtml.

3. *Archbishop Desmond Tutu with Bill Moyers*, VHS (Princeton, NJ: Films for the Humanities and Sciences, 1999).

4. Desmond Tutu, *Crying in the Wilderness: The Struggle for Justice in South Africa* (Grand Rapids, MI: William B. Eerdmans, 1990), p. 93.

5. Desmond Tutu, in discussion with the author, 29 April 2003, Jacksonville, FL.

6. Archbishop Desmond Tutu, interview at the Hall of Public Service, 2 May 2003, Washington, DC, www.achievement.org/autodoc/page/tut0int-1.

7. Christopher Matthews, "The Prayers of Desmond Tutu," *San Francisco Examiner*, 1 May 1994.

8. Adrian Hadland, *Desmond Tutu*, They Fought for Freedom Series (Cape Town: Maskew Miller Longman, 2001), p. 7.

9. For more on Tutu's childhood (and his life up to 1987), see Shirley du Boulay, *Tutu: Voice of the Voiceless* (Grand Rapids, MI: William B. Eerdmans, 1988).

Chapter 2

YOUTH

As both a youth and an adult, Desmond Tutu rarely stayed in one place for very long. In 1943, when Desmond was 12, the Tutus moved to Krugersdorp, just northwest of Roodepoort. Zachariah had been transferred to yet another school. The family settled in Munsieville, Krugersdorp's black township. Munsieville's neighborhoods lacked paved roads and electricity, although the Tutus' three-room house did have running water and a bathroom. Desmond slept in the family's living room and eating area. Like most black South African families, the Tutus struggled to get by on meager resources. Zachariah supplemented his income by delivering bottles during the Christmas holidays; Aletha resumed washing clothes for white families.

Looking back on his youth years later, Tutu would describe himself as a "township urchin." He often went without shoes and was once accosted by a police officer who suspected he was homeless or a beggar. To earn extra money, Desmond and his friend Joe Sibiya would walk four miles to a market and bring back oranges to sell in their neighborhood. Desmond also sold peanuts and fruit at a railway station and caddied at the Killarney golf course in the wealthy Johannesburg suburb of Houghton. But not all of his time was spent working. Desmond joined a Boy Scout troop in a town eight miles from Munsieville and eventually earned several merit badges. Meritorious Boy Scout though he was, Tutu is the first to admit that he was not a saint as a youth. When his father gave him his monthly allowance, he would sometimes use the money to buy cigarettes.[1]

In 1945, Desmond enrolled at Western Native Township High School, the only public high school for Africans in the western area of Johannesburg. Students came from all over the Witwatersrand to attend the school. Desmond stood out on his first day of class not only because he was small for his age, but also because he was barefoot and wore shorts. Getting to school on time proved difficult because he lived 15 miles away. At first he took the train to school, but when commuting from Munsieville became too expensive, he moved into a dormitory run by the Community of the Resurrection in Sophiatown. The Community of the Resurrection was an Anglican religious order whose priests took special vows of poverty, chastity, and obedience. Members of this order ministered to Africans throughout the Johannesburg area and offered accommodation to African students in need. At one point Desmond also stayed with an aunt and uncle who lived closer to his high school.

Western Native Township High School offered a broad range of classes, including Latin, English, chemistry, physics, mathematics, and history. The facilities, like those at most black schools, were poor and overcrowded. Classes had approximately 60 students each, and a church hall was used for four different classes at once. In that environment, Tutu later recalled, "the one who shouted the loudest tended to get the most attention."[2] Most students had to make do without desks. When a hard surface to write on was needed, the seat of a bench became a makeshift desktop. The school lacked adequate scientific equipment as well. In fact, Tutu remembered going to a laboratory only once in high school. In history class, the textbooks presented South African history solely from a white perspective. They made it seem as if Africans "stole" cattle from white settlers, while never suggesting that the whites also seized African property. During breaks in the school day, Desmond and his fellow students had to fend for themselves because no school meals were furnished. Luckily, Desmond's parents gave him enough money to buy small snacks in nearby Sophiatown, such as peanuts, bread, and flavored water.

Teachers at the school sought to keep morale high despite the inadequate learning environment. The principal, Harry Madibane, was known for being a stickler about punctuality and the personal appearance of his students. He was quite strict, Tutu remembered, "but he imbued you with a pride." As students, "we didn't go around feeling sorry for ourselves," he continued. He and his classmates took some of the same exams as white students and could do as well as or better than the whites. The teachers urged their students to aim high and not become demoralized by the squalor, deprivation, and poverty that surrounded them.[3] Apparently, Desmond took this message to heart. He earned high marks in his classes and impressed both his teachers and his classmates with his academic ability.

Desmond's best friend in this era was Stanley Motjuwadi, whom he met on his first day of high school. The two became inseparable as they took the train together to school each morning. To pass the time, Stanley and Desmond played cards with their fellow commuters. One of their favorite games was "five card." They soon worked out a system of hand signals to cheat unsuspecting passengers. For example, if one boy scratched his chest, that meant "hearts;" other signals indicated other suits.[4] The boys' antics as card sharks earned them some extra money—and the grudging respect of their fellow passengers. Some of the commuters even began referring to Desmond as "the professor."[5] His friend Stanley was as gifted in the classroom as he was. Tutu later recalled that Stanley would play golf while his friends were studying and then review his friends' notes just before examinations. Stanley passed all of his subjects whereas some of his friends failed. He would eventually become editor of *Drum* magazine, one of the most widely read black South African publications in the country. He would be Desmond Tutu's closest friend for the next 50 years.

Desmond's high school career was suddenly interrupted in 1945, when at the age of 14, he was diagnosed with tuberculosis (TB). He had always been a thin, frail youngster, but this was the most serious illness of his life. He was sent to Rietfontein Hospital on Johannesburg's east side for treatment. Although he could not have imagined it at the time, he would remain in the hospital for the next 20 months. His illness, the surroundings of the hospital, and the treatment he underwent made this an extraordinarily difficult period for Desmond. At one point he began coughing blood, which greatly alarmed his doctors. Desmond feared that his days were numbered. Although he eventually recovered, he experienced intense feelings of isolation, loneliness, and despair during his long convalescence.

Helping Desmond cope with the long, lonely days in the hospital was the Anglican priest Trevor Huddleston. He was the man who had tipped his hat to Desmond's mother a few years earlier in Roodepoort. Father Huddleston had arrived from England in 1943 after joining the Community of the Resurrection. Upon arrival in South Africa he was put in charge of Christ the King Church in Sophiatown. Soon he developed a stellar reputation among his flock of black South African Anglicans, especially young people. Once he learned of Desmond's illness, he began to visit the boy every weekend to chat and bring him books. Thanks to Father Huddleston, Desmond read voraciously during his hospitalization, going through his schoolbooks and devouring classics such as *Treasure Island* and *Oliver Twist*. He even accumulated a large collection of comic books, especially titles such as *Superman* and *Batman*. Not only did Father

Huddleston provide comfort and companionship, but he discussed the problems of South African society with Desmond frankly and openly. Desmond was overwhelmed by the man's kindness. "I was just a nonentity," Tutu recalled, "and yet he paid so much attention to me."[6]

Trevor Huddleston later shared his own memories about Desmond in the book *Hope and Suffering*, a collection of Tutu's writings and sermons:

> I have had the privilege of knowing Desmond Tutu for the best part of forty years. Our friendship began when he was a small boy and I was a young and inexperienced priest with the responsibility for a vast African parish in Johannesburg. It grew and deepened when he had to spend long and weary months in hospital, and I would visit him and take him books to read, and always I would leave his bedside refreshed and cheered. The suffering was there all right because, with that exceptional intelligence and important exams awaiting him, he was frustrated and not a little lonely. But it was the hope that carried him so triumphantly through, and helped to carry me through with him. Those days and those visits are amongst my most precious memories of what was, for me, the golden age of my whole ministry.[7]

Father Huddleston was destined to become a legendary figure in South African history. He helped rally opposition to the South African government's plans to destroy multiracial neighborhoods and downgrade black education in the 1950s. He then wrote the book *Naught for Your Comfort*, an eloquent account of his ministry in South Africa that exposed the intensity of suffering and racial discrimination in the country. Although he was forced to leave South Africa in the late 1950s, he eventually became the leader of the British antiapartheid movement. His dedication to freedom and justice for all earned him the highest honor from the African National Congress, the main African civil rights group in South Africa. His passionate advocacy of black South African rights was exceptional in an era when most white South Africans fully supported racial discrimination. This towering example of Christian compassion would become the most important influence in Desmond Tutu's life.

Desmond's Christian faith deepened during his long hospitalization for TB. This was in large part due to the inspiring example of Father Huddleston, a man of boundless courage and caring. Referring to his mentor years later, Tutu wrote, "We just want to thank God so very much for the wonderful, wonderful person who made us blacks realize that not all whites were the same.... And if blacks still talk to white people, an extraordinary miracle in present-day South Africa, then it will be in large measure due to people like Trevor, who made us realize that we too count, we too matter in the sight of God."[8] No longer just a Christian on the surface, Desmond embraced Christianity with his very soul while a patient. Once he recovered from his illness, he made his first sacramental confession to Father Huddleston at Christ the King Church in Sophiatown. He then became a server—the Anglican equivalent of an altar boy—at St. Paul's Church in Munsieville.

After Desmond's release from the hospital, he remained isolated at home for a short period. The most serious aftereffect of his long illness was the partial paralysis of his right hand. To compensate for this condition, he became left-handed and developed the habit of rubbing his hands together periodically. In all other respects Desmond regained his health and returned to normal activity at home and at school. Despite his absence from classes for more than a year and a half, he picked up where he left off and eventually earned his junior certificate after completing the equivalent of 10th grade. He also resumed commuting to school from Munsieville. During his last two years of high school he had a wonderful teacher for English literature, Geoff Mamabulu. "He really was quite extraordinary," Tutu remembered more than 50 years later. "When he spoke of a Shakespearean play, you almost thought that he grew up with Shakespeare!"[9] Tutu's love of literature would remain with him for the rest of his life.

As a teenager, Desmond was inspired not only by some fine teachers and Father Huddleston's Christian compassion, but also by the achievements of black Americans. The United States began taking tentative steps away from racial segregation in the late 1940s, particularly in the army and major-league baseball. Sometime after he recovered from TB, Desmond found a tattered copy of *Ebony* magazine that described how Jackie Robinson had broken the color line in major-league baseball in 1947. "Now I didn't know baseball from ping-pong," Tutu admitted, but he was tremendously impressed that a black man could overcome such overwhelming odds and ultimately triumph. Desmond was determined to succeed in his country as well, despite the obstacles facing black South Africans.[10] He was inspired by other black American athletes who had realized their dreams, such as the boxers Joe Louis and Sugar Ray Robinson. Desmond and his friends had also heard about the earlier achievements of Jesse Owens, the black American track star who stunned Adolf Hitler by winning four gold medals at the 1936 Olympic games in Berlin. That feat had demolished the myth of white racial supremacy in the eyes of both black Americans and black South Africans. Black American entertainers also captivated Desmond and his friends. They listened to the music of Nat King Cole, Louis Armstrong, Fats Waller, Marian Anderson, and Lena Horne.

At the end of 1950, when he was 19 years old, Desmond finished high school and passed the Joint Matriculation Board exams. He was one of only 0.5 percent of Africans who qualified for university entrance in South Africa that year.[11] The time had come for Desmond to make some important decisions about his future. Early in his high school career, he had dreamed of attending Fort Hare, the only university fully open to Africans in South Africa. His father hoped he would go into teaching; Desmond originally planned to become a doctor. He was partly inspired by the example of Dr. Alfred B. Xuma, the first western-trained African physician to practice medicine in Johannesburg. This Sophiatown doctor was one of black South Africa's greatest role models for high academic and professional achievement in the 1940s. Another reason behind Desmond's interest in medicine was his desire to research TB, which had so devastated his own health as a youth. He was admitted to medical school at the University of the Witwatersrand in Johannesburg, but his family could not afford to pay his tuition there. Because no scholarship materialized, Desmond was forced to make other plans. Then, much to his father's satisfaction, he decided to become a teacher. He enrolled at Bantu Normal College near Pretoria in 1951 to begin studying for a teacher's diploma. As Desmond contemplated his own future, the future for black South Africans looked increasingly bleak.

NOTES

1. Shirley du Boulay, *Tutu: Voice of the Voiceless* (Grand Rapids, MI: William B. Eerdmans, 1988), p. 28.

2. Desmond Tutu, in discussion with the author, 29 April 2003, Jacksonville, FL.

3. Desmond Tutu, in discussion with the author.

4. Adrian Hadland, *Desmond Tutu*, They Fought for Freedom Series (Cape Town: Maskew Miller Longman, 2001), pp. 9–10.

5. David Winner, *Desmond Tutu*, People Who Helped the World Series (Harrisburg, PA: Morehouse, 1989), p. 16.

6. Desmond Tutu, "An Appreciation of the Rt. Revd Trevor Huddleston, CR," in *Trevor Huddleston: Essays on his Life and Work*, ed. Deborah Duncan Honore (New York: Oxford University Press, 1988), p. 4.

7. Trevor Huddleston, "Foreword" in Desmond Tutu, *Hope and Suffering* (Grand Rapids, MI: William B. Eerdmans, 1984), p. 9.

8. Tutu, "An Appreciation," pp. 3–4.

9. Archbishop Desmond Tutu, interview at the Hall of Public Service, 2 May 2003, Washington, DC, www.achievement.org/autodoc/page/tut0int-1.

10. Desmond Tutu, "Great Conversations" (lecture, University of Minnesota–Twin Cities, 25 February 2003), www.news.mpr.org/programs/midday/listings/md20030303.shtml.

11. Du Boulay, *Tutu,* pp. 35–36.

Chapter 3

TEACHING IN A LAND OF APARTHEID

The year 1948 marked a turning point in South African history. In that year, the newly elected National Party led by Daniel F. Malan took office and signaled its determination to widen the gulf between the country's racial groups. The African majority had no voting rights and viewed the 1948 election results with alarm. The victorious Nationalists, most of whom were Afrikaners, called their policy "apartheid," which is the Afrikaans word for "separateness." Prime Minister Malan believed that an accelerated program of racial separateness would protect the interests of the white minority. Racial segregation in South Africa was not new, of course, but after 1948, it was intensified as never before. Apartheid would create great turmoil at home and generate unprecedented controversy abroad for the next 45 years. Desmond Tutu would eventually dedicate much of his adult life to ending this legalized system of racial discrimination.

Shortly after it took office, the National Party began to enact new laws separating the races in all areas of South African life. The Prohibition of Mixed Marriages Act (1949) and the Immorality Act (1950) prohibited marriage and sexual relations between citizens of different races. The Population Registration Act (1950) required all South Africans to be classified by race at birth. The government-assigned racial classification would shape a person's entire life—where they could go to school, whom they could marry, where they could live and work, what political rights (if any) they could exercise, even where they could be buried. The Group Areas Act (1950) intensified the segregation of South Africa's urban areas. This act prohibited whites, Africans, Indians, and mixed-race citizens from living in neighborhoods with different racial groups. The Suppression of Communism Act (1950) not only made the Communist Party illegal, but it gave the government the right to prohibit a wide spectrum of opposition. The Bantu Education Act (1953) created a separate system of inferior education for the African majority. The Reservation of Separate Amenities Act (1953) segregated most public areas in South Africa, such as cinemas, hotels, restaurants, restrooms, hospitals, buses, and trains. It even sanctioned whites-only beaches and park benches. Under apartheid, African men were still required to carry passes at all times; by the late 1950s, African women were required to do so as well. All of these laws—and many more—made South Africa the most racially polarized nation on Earth.

Some South Africans were determined to resist the new apartheid measures, even if it meant going to jail. In 1952, antiapartheid activists organized a defiance campaign to break unjust laws. Volunteers began ignoring apartheid regulations in several cities that year, such as those that segregated public areas and imposed curfews. The government reacted by imposing harsh penalties for civil disobedience, but opponents of apartheid vowed to fight on. By the mid-1950s, activists representing all of South Africa's races pledged to intensify their cooperation in the struggle against racial discrimination.

Desmond Tutu began his teacher training just as the apartheid system was being implemented. He enrolled at Pretoria's Bantu Normal College in 1951. Pretoria was South Africa's administrative capital and the citadel of apartheid. Like the city itself, the college had a heavy Afrikaner presence. Although all of the students were African, most of the college's administrators and instructors were Afrikaners who fully supported apartheid. The dormitories and classrooms at the college were grass-thatched rondavels (round huts), because the Afrikaner administrators believed that this architectural style reflected the culture of the African students. "They said we ought to develop along our own lines," Tutu recalled 30 years later. "They said rectangular buildings weren't good for the black psyche."[1] Rectangular classrooms were only constructed when the college's biology instructor complained that the lack of light in the rondavels made working with microscopes difficult.

Tutu was quite popular with his classmates at the college. His best friend, Stanley Motjuwadi, was a fellow student, as was a new friend, Stanley Mogoba. According to Mogoba, Tutu was one of the best students at the college, especially in English. One English instructor discouraged African students from using long and complex words in their assignments, but he made an exception for Tutu and one other student because their

English was so good. Mogoba marveled at Tutu's remarkable memory and rich sense of humor. Years later he recalled a humorous classroom anecdote involving his friend: "One of our teachers whose English was very fragmentary and who translated literally from Afrikaans to English (for example, 'Students, you must remember me to show you a diagram') made one of these cracks in class. We all suppressed ourselves. Someone kicked Desmond from under the table and he exploded [with laughter]. He was sent out of class for a few days."[2] One weekend Tutu invited Mogoba to come home with him to Munsieville to visit his family. Mogoba accepted the invitation and observed that Tutu's family spoke both Xhosa and Sotho. "This was a typical African family which gave birth to a son who became truly African," Mogoba later wrote. Desmond's ease with language showed that he had "no sign of any ethnicity about him."[3]

Tutu's leadership qualities manifested themselves when his fellow students elected him to the students' representative council at his college. He also became chairman of the college debating society. At one point Tutu and his peers went to Johannesburg to engage in a debate with students at the Jan Hofmeyr School of Social Work. The judge of the debate was none other than Nelson Mandela, a young lawyer and antiapartheid activist in the African National Congress. Tutu and Mandela met at the debate, neither imagining that they would both become icons of South African freedom in the decades to come.

Tutu continued to value his friendship with Trevor Huddleston. On one occasion he invited Father Huddleston to Pretoria to speak at the college on the relevance of religion to social problems. Both students and faculty attended the lecture. Following the talk, the principal of the college, who was an Afrikaner and a member of the Dutch Reformed Church, invited Father Huddleston to tea at his house. Huddleston agreed and was accompanied by an African chaplain and an African teacher. Although the principal was hospitable, he was puzzled that his guest had tried to link Christianity with South African race relations. He had tea with Huddleston in one room of the house, while the African priest and teacher were served in another. The apartheid mentality had clearly permeated Tutu's college by the early 1950s.

Tutu was not overtly political as an education student, nor were most of his peers. They did not engage in strikes or boycotts, but they were deeply troubled by South Africa's divided society. Some of Tutu's fellow education students were becoming increasingly bitter over apartheid. Tutu focused on his studies and earned his teacher's diploma in 1953.

In 1954, Tutu began his teaching career at his old high school, which had become known as Madibane High School in honor of its principal.

He commuted to Western Native Township from Munsieville, just as he had done years before. At night, Tutu studied for his bachelor's degree by correspondence from the University of South Africa (UNISA), which was based in Pretoria. His subjects included Zulu, sociology, English, history, biology, and the history of education. While studying for his degree, Tutu met Robert Sobukwe, an instructor of African languages at the University of the Witwatersrand in Johannesburg. Sobukwe would become one of the most prominent black South African political leaders in the late 1950s. Tutu was impressed by Sobukwe's intellect and principles but did not join his political activities. His work as a full-time teacher and a full-time university student absorbed all of his energies. He earned his BA from UNISA at the end of 1954.

Just as Tutu was launching his teaching career, he also began a courtship. During his college days in Pretoria he had become attracted to a young woman who walked by his classroom each morning. Her name was Leah Nomalizo Shenxane, another education student at the college. Tutu had first met Leah during his high school days, when she had befriended his younger sister, Gloria. Leah had been a student in one of Zachariah's classes as a child and also lived in Munsieville. She had always thought of Desmond as being a bit conceited, but when she got to know him better in college, she became captivated by his intelligence and sense of humor. The two grew closer after Tutu started teaching. Then they decided to get married. Had Leah not accepted Tutu's proposal, he probably would have eventually joined the Community of the Resurrection, the celibate religious order of which Trevor Huddleston was a member. Desmond and Leah were married on July 2, 1955; Tutu's best friend Stanley Motjuwadi was his best man. Tutu would later joke that he and his wife's first home was the living room/dining room in his parents' house.[4]

When a new high school opened in Munsieville shortly after the Tutus were married, Desmond was hired to teach there. He taught a variety of subjects, including math, Afrikaans, and English. It was not unusual for classes to have 60 students, whose ages could range from 14 to 27. Tutu's enthusiasm in the classroom won him the admiration of many students. He displayed a special talent for teaching literature and writing. One of the challenges Tutu faced was using the Eurocentric textbooks his students were issued without perpetuating racial or cultural stereotypes. When these textbooks did cover Africans, they invariably did so from a white perspective. Gangs could also be a problem at the school. During one incident, Tutu seized a gun from gang members who had disrupted his class, while the school principal hid in his office.[5]

The increasingly harsh nature of apartheid became evident early in Tutu's teaching career. In the 1950s, the Nationalist government began to advocate the destruction of Sophiatown, the Johannesburg neighborhood in which Trevor Huddleston's Christ the King Church was located. Tutu had a connection to Sophiatown as well; he had lived temporarily at the Community of the Resurrection's hostel there during high school. Sophiatown was home to approximately 60,000 people by the early 1950s. Africans, Indians, and mixed-race citizens both owned and rented property there. Sophiatown was a few miles west of downtown Johannesburg. Its location, plus the possibility of owning property, made it a desirable neighborhood for blacks, who could often find accommodation only in more strictly controlled townships, if anywhere at all. As Sophiatown's popularity surged, so did its population.

The Nationalist government labeled Sophiatown a "black spot" because it had become surrounded by white suburbs. Intent on implementing apartheid in Johannesburg's western areas, government officials decided to force all 60,000 Sophiatown residents to move to segregated townships farther away from the city center. Once the neighborhood was cleared of all blacks, the government planned to build a white suburb in its place, intentionally destroying African property rights in the process. The government viewed Africans as only temporary urban dwellers. As long as they fulfilled their role as manual laborers in the white-dominated economy, they would be allowed to rent property in urban townships. When they ceased being "useful," the government reserved the right to revoke their temporary residence rights. In the words of Native Affairs Minister Hendrik Verwoerd, "The African is in town to work. That is his function. If he desires a fuller life and a sense of belonging, then he must go to the Reserves."[6] Reserves were scattered rural territories allocated on an ethnic basis on which Africans could own land. These reserves represented only about 13 percent of South Africa's total land mass and never satisfied the political or economic aspirations of most black South Africans.

Trevor Huddleston, the African National Congress, and many Sophiatown residents opposed the government's removal plan, but their resistance campaign failed. The government forced the first Sophiatown residents to leave in early 1955. Their property was loaded onto trucks and taken to outlying areas earmarked for Africans, Indians, and Coloureds. During the next few years the government demolished most of the homes and vacant buildings in Sophiatown. They named the new, white suburb built on the ruins of Sophiatown "Triomf" (Afrikaans for *triumph*). The destruction of Sophiatown received widespread media coverage all over the world, especially in the United States, which was experiencing its own battles over racial segregation at the same time. In South Africa, the future of race relations looked very grim indeed.

Another aspect of apartheid affected Desmond Tutu more directly in these years—Bantu education. Literally "people" in the Nguni languages of South Africa, *bantu* was a term used by the Nationalist government to refer to all Africans in South Africa, and Bantu education was the public schooling that its regime provided for them. This form of inferior education represented a serious threat to the already fragile state of African education in South Africa. Before the apartheid era, only one in three African youths attended school at a given time, and most only completed a few early grades. There was no compulsory education for Africans in South Africa; the government channeled its resources into white schools, not black schools. Church-run missionary institutions provided the bulk of African education before the Bantu education policy was developed. In 1945, there were more than 4,000 missionary schools but only 230 government schools for Africans.[7] Some of the mission schools, such as St. Peter's, Adams, and Lovedale, had long-standing traditions of excellence. Although they ran the majority of African schools, the churches did not have enough resources to accommodate all of the African children who wanted to attend.

The Bantu Education Act passed in 1953 and was implemented two years later. The brainchild of Native Affairs Minister Verwoerd, this act outlined a new system of downgraded education for Africans. Verwoerd believed that the education the missionaries offered gave Africans false hopes. "What is the use of teaching the Bantu child mathematics when it cannot use it in practice?" he asked. "If the Native in South Africa today is being taught to expect that he will live his adult life under a policy of equal rights, he is making a big mistake."[8]

After the passage of the Bantu Education Act, the government presented mission schools with an ultimatum. They could either transfer control of their schools to the government or they could retain control and lose all government subsidies. Given the precarious financial position of most mission schools, they could ill afford the latter alternative. Bantu education thus all but ended missionary influence in African education. Not only did the government assume control over most African schools, but these schools would be administered by the Department of Native Affairs, not the Department of Education. From now on, education would be designed to prepare Africans for subservient positions in South African society, not give them the same qualifications or skills as whites. Schools for Africans would get a curriculum separate from white schools, one that focused on manual labor and vocational training rather than math, science, or university preparation. The Bantu Education Act also required African schools to emphasize the teaching of African languages, not English. In short, the new policy was specifically designed to educate Africans for inferiority.

Trevor Huddleston labeled the government's new policy "education for servitude." He predicted that "its consequences will be so grave for the African people that they may take a generation or more to recover from them."[9] He and his Anglican colleagues decided to close St. Peter's College rather than surrender control to the government. Huddleston knew that black South Africans would never accept such an inferior system of education and he was right. Most African political organizations vehemently opposed Bantu education. The ANC advocated a total boycott of all government-run schools for Africans. Not only did many students participate in the boycott, but some parents even started holding alternative classes in their homes. Then Verwoerd issued another ultimatum: students had to return to school immediately or they would be barred from school permanently. Eventually students began to trickle back to their schools, but their resentment over Bantu education did not diminish.

The Bantu Education Act was implemented during Tutu's second year of teaching. He became alarmed when he saw the new syllabus for African schools proposed by the government. In his eyes, it was far too simple and thin. He knew immediately that he could not support such a system. Dedicated though he was to his students, Tutu did not want to train them for inferiority. He decided to leave teaching in 1958, just three years after Bantu education was introduced. His wife, Leah, resigned her teaching post as well. The Tutus were not the only ones facing such a painful decision. Many black South Africans left the teaching profession in this era "because they could no longer realize the goals they had set for their pupils."[10] Had it not been for Bantu education, the Tutus and many other talented African teachers would have remained in the profession.

Tutu's father was greatly disappointed when Desmond announced he was leaving teaching. Zachariah had encouraged his son to become a teacher in the first place and hoped he would stay in the field despite Bantu education. He thought Desmond stood a good chance of becoming the headmaster of Munsieville High School one day. Some of Desmond's former students were also disappointed by his decision, but Tutu had made up his mind. Tutu's strong stand on behalf of his principles resembled that taken by his mentor, Trevor Huddleston. Father Huddleston did not want to compromise with Bantu education by keeping St. Peter's open; Tutu did not want to compromise with the policy by continuing to teach. Both men were devout Christians who refused to acquiesce in the face of apartheid.

There was a bright spot for Tutu during these years of disenchantment—his family. Just a year after the implementation of Bantu education, Desmond and Leah had a baby son on April 14, 1956. They named the boy Trevor, after Trevor Huddleston. "When I became a father for the first time I was so proud and happy," Tutu said. "It made me feel a little like God."[11] Desmond and Leah would have another child in the late 1950s, this time a girl named Theresa. Two more daughters, Naomi and Mpho, would be born in the early 1960s. Now that he was leaving teaching, Desmond Tutu had to find a way to provide for his growing family. He decided to do so by becoming a priest.

NOTES

1. Quoted in Joseph Lelyveld, "South Africa's Bishop Tutu," *New York Times Magazine*, 14 March 1982, p. 44.

2. Mmutlanyane Stanley Mogoba, "From Munsieville to Oslo," in *Hammering Swords Into Ploughshares: Essays in Honor of Archbishop Mpilo Desmond Tutu*, ed. Buti Tlhagale and Itumeleng Mosala (Grand Rapids, MI: William B. Eerdmans, 1987), p. 24.

3. Mogoba, "From Munsieville to Oslo," p. 25.

4. Mothobi Mutloatse, "Mutloatse on Tutu," *Ecunews* 8 (December 1984): p. 17.

5. Shirley du Boulay, *Tutu: Voice of the Voiceless* (Grand Rapids, MI: William B. Eerdmans, 1988), p. 40.

6. Quoted in Trevor Huddleston, *Naught for Your Comfort* (Garden City, NY: Doubleday, 1956), p. 52.

7. Huddleston, *Naught for Your Comfort*, p. 160.

8. Quoted in David Winner, *Desmond Tutu*, People Who Helped the World Series (Harrisburg, PA: Morehouse, 1989), p. 20.

9. Huddleston, *Naught for Your Comfort*, p. 158.

10. Rosemary Mulholland, *South Africa, 1948–1994* (New York: Cambridge University Press, 1997), p. 33.

11. Adrian Hadland, *Desmond Tutu*, They Fought for Freedom Series (Cape Town: Maskew Miller Longman, 2001), p. 14.

Chapter 4

ENTERING THE PRIESTHOOD

Although it took his father by surprise, Desmond Tutu's decision to enter the priesthood made perfect sense. His decision stemmed from both his strong religious faith and his belief that the priesthood was "another form of service close in many ways to that of a teacher."[1] One of his grandfathers had been a minister of an African independent church; Desmond himself had been a committed Christian since his boyhood. His early role models as a youth had been Father Sekgaphane, his first Anglican priest, and Trevor Huddleston. Father Huddleston had consistently spoken out on behalf of the poor and the oppressed, greatly inspiring Desmond. As an adult, even before he contemplated theological training, Tutu served as a subdeacon at his Munsieville church, which gave him special responsibilities regarding communion, readings, and the church choir. He believed that the priesthood would allow him to continue to serve his people. Tutu later referred to his decision to enter the ministry as "God grabbing me by the scruff of my neck."[2]

Tutu's father wasn't the only one mystified by his son's career change; some of Desmond's friends and former students were also taken aback by his decision. They believed that the churches had done little to improve the plight of black South Africans. They also knew of Tutu's great potential as an educator and feared that his intellectual skills would be wasted in the priesthood. The reaction of Stanley Mogoba, a friend from teacher training college, was typical: "We heard rumors that Desmond had responded to a call to the ministry. Many of his former friends were disappointed in him. Why did he not remain as an English teacher and later become a professor of English? Some of us felt that perhaps Father Huddleston had had a hand in this. Little did we know that some of us, after taking a circuitous route, would also heed a call from God."[3] Coincidentally, Mogoba also left teaching eventually and became a leading minister in the Methodist Church of South Africa.

Like schools, churches also reflected the problems of South African society. African ministers faced discrimination from the white-controlled church structures in terms of both pay and advancement opportunities. Whites dominated the leadership positions in most Christian churches with missionary roots. African clergymen, while respected by their communities, generally occupied a lower status than did African teachers. Black South Africans were not freely welcomed in most white churches, and under apartheid, this tendency intensified.

In 1957, the Nationalist government launched a formal effort to impose apartheid on churches. It began drafting legislation that would make it difficult for different races to worship together at the same church. Specifically, clause 20c of the Native Laws Amendment Bill was designed to restrict black church attendance in white areas. The first draft of the clause stated that churches in white areas could not admit Africans unless the churches received special permission from the minister of native affairs and local authorities. This applied to all services, meetings, and gatherings at churches in white neighborhoods.

The bill aroused immediate opposition from leaders of the so-called English-speaking churches in South Africa (Anglican, Catholic, Congregational, Methodist, Presbyterian). South Africa's most famous writer, Alan Paton, wrote, "Was a state, purporting to be Christian, empowered by God to forbid the Christian Church to admit any person...on grounds of his race?"[4] The Anglican archbishop of Cape Town, Geoffrey Clayton, warned Prime Minister J. G. Strijdom that the church law would not be obeyed. He and many of his fellow church leaders viewed it as an unacceptable infringement upon religious freedom. Clayton, then in his early seventies, realized that he might be forced to break the law if the government refused to back down. He didn't live long enough to find out. A day after drafting and signing a letter of protest, Archbishop Clayton collapsed and died of a heart attack in his Cape Town residence.

After the firestorm over the church clause erupted, the government decided to amend the bill. It backed away from its initial requirement that white churches apply for permission to accommodate black worshippers. Instead, the government reserved the right to prohibit African worship at such churches. The second draft of the bill said that the native affairs minister would prohibit African attendance at a white church only if it created a "nuisance." If the prohibition was announced and violated, the offending African(s) would be prosecuted, not the church. The amended bill passed in mid-1957.

Most church leaders still refused to accept the government's plan. Anglican leaders instructed their churches to disregard the law, believing that it still violated religious freedom. As it turned out, the church clause was never enforced. Mixed congregations occasionally worshipped together in large cities, where strenuous objections were rare. Mixed services in small towns and rural areas were virtually unheard of. Nevertheless, the English-speaking churches' opposition to the church clause was a proud moment for them. It showed that they could be true to their convictions, even if it meant angering the apartheid government.

Tutu began his theological training just as the church clause was being enacted. In 1958, he left Munsieville High School and entered the Anglican-run St. Peter's Theological College in Rosettenville, Johannesburg. Trevor Huddleston and the Community of the Resurrection had closed down the secondary school at St. Peter's after the Bantu Education Act was implemented, but the theological school remained open. Tutu began studying for the licentiate of theology, the more advanced of the college's two theological courses. The licentiate course lasted three years. Tutu distinguished himself as a student at St. Peter's, earning high marks in subjects such as the Old and New Testament, church history, and Greek. His instructors were thoroughly impressed by his abilities. Tutu's fellow students remembered him as an outgoing, caring soul with a wonderful sense of humor.

Tutu embraced the values of the Community of the Resurrection, especially its identification with the oppressed. Priests in the community believed that their spirituality had to address attitudes and conditions in South Africa's racially divided society. They preached the need to love one's neighbor, even if the neighbor did not reciprocate. The person whom Tutu admired most at St. Peter's was the vice-principal, Father Timothy Stanton. Father Stanton drew no distinction between the races or between himself and his students. As Tutu recalled, "I remember how I was amazed that he, the vice principal, and a white man to boot, would join the black students in doing some of the menial tasks in the college."[5] In Tutu's eyes, Father Stanton was "truly saintly."[6] Tutu also admired the community's stress on prayer and meditation. As a student at St. Peter's, Tutu internalized the need for regular retreats and meditations, often performing his own daily meditation before sunrise. He would continue this habit for years to come.

In his third and final year at St. Peter's, Tutu was appointed "senior student," an honorary position that reflected his leadership qualities and his ability to make all feel welcome at the college. Absorbed as he was in his studies, Tutu was not politically active at this stage. He did follow the major political developments of the day, such as the Treason Trial, in which the government charged leading antiapartheid activists with planning a violent insurrection against the state. During this trial, which lasted from 1956 until 1961, two of the most prominent accused met with some students at St. Peter's, including Tutu. The men were Albert Lutuli and Z. K. Matthews, widely respected leaders of the ANC. Although Tutu had not yet participated in the antiapartheid movement himself, he admired Lutuli and Matthews and wished there were more leaders of their caliber in South Africa. Eventually, charges were dropped against each of the Treason Trial's original 156 accused, or they were found not guilty.

Perhaps the only element of St. Peter's that frustrated Tutu was the college's rule that its students could not live with their wives until after graduation. Desmond and Leah had no choice but to live apart for a time. Having left teaching herself because of Bantu education, Leah decided to train as a nurse while Desmond's mother cared for the couple's children. In 1960, Desmond was awarded the licentiate of theology from St. Peter's with two distinctions. He felt deeply indebted to the Community of the Resurrection for the guidance and theological training it offered him. Years later, he called his debt to the community "incalculable."[7]

The political situation in South Africa had sharply deteriorated by the time Tutu completed his studies at St. Peter's. Native Affairs Minister Hendrik Verwoerd, known to many as the "architect of apartheid," had become prime minister in 1958. His determination to expand apartheid generated a new wave of resistance among black South Africans. In March 1960, the Pan Africanist Congress (PAC) launched a series of antipass demonstrations all over South Africa involving thousands of eager volunteers. PAC leader Robert Sobukwe called passes "the distinctive badge of slavery and humiliation for black South Africans."[8] He encouraged his followers to leave home without their passes on a designated day and congregate at police stations in protest. On March 21, 1960, several thousand antipass demonstrators gathered at the police station in Sharpeville, a black township south of Johannesburg. Without warning, the police opened fire on the crowd, killing at least 69 people and wounding 180, including women and children. Most of the victims were shot in the back as they tried to flee. This massacre sent shock waves throughout South Africa and the rest of the world.

Nine days after the Sharpeville tragedy, a crowd estimated at 30,000 marched from Cape Town's black townships to the city center to protest the recent shootings. Anger over apartheid had clearly reached unprecedented levels. Mass disaffection permeated the black community, while fear swept through white South Africa. To some it appeared as if the country was on the brink of a revolution. In the days that followed, a new period of repression began in South Africa. The government declared a state of emergency, banned the ANC and the PAC, ordered the detention without trial of hundreds of people, and jailed Robert Sobukwe on Robben Island, the notorious prison off the coast of Cape Town. In order to escape the government's crackdown, many antiapartheid activists went into exile overseas. Others vowed to continue the struggle at home no matter what the cost.

The whole world seemed to criticize apartheid following the Sharpeville tragedy. In the words of a recent historian of the massacre, the world's "distaste for apartheid turned to horror."[9] Soon an international movement to isolate South Africa began. The South African economy was shaken as foreign investment dried up temporarily. Angry over the world's condemnation of his government, Verwoerd urged white voters to approve a referendum calling for South Africa to cut its ties with Britain and become a republic. They did so, and South Africa formally left the British Commonwealth on May 31, 1961.

After the ANC and the PAC were banned, their leaders were forced either underground or into exile. Some activists believed that peaceful protest had become futile and that their only option was to embark on an armed struggle. The decision to take up arms was a momentous one for the ANC in particular, since it had been committed to nonviolent protest since its founding in 1912. As South Africa became more polarized after Sharpeville, the pass laws continued to be enforced. They would remain in effect until 1986.

Tutu was in this third and last year at St. Peter's when the Sharpeville tragedy occurred. He knew Robert Sobukwe, the man whose organization had coordinated the antipass demonstrations. Tutu heard about the shootings on the radio and felt a deep sense of shock, sadness, and helplessness. In the days following the massacre, he admired the stand taken by Ambrose Reeves, the white Anglican bishop of Johannesburg. Bishop Reeves not only condemned the police actions at Sharpeville, but he led the public outcry over the shootings and demanded that the government open a commission of inquiry into the tragedy. He visited the injured in the hospital and collected first-hand testimony about what happened in the township. He also helped assemble a legal team to represent the interests of the victims and their families. Just as Trevor Huddleston had done a few years earlier, Bishop Reeves warned that the government's apartheid policy was destined to bring tragedy to South Africa. Within a year of the Sharpeville incident, Reeves was deported from South Africa and never allowed to return.

Nine months after Sharpeville, Tutu was ordained as a deacon at a ceremony at St. Mary's Cathedral in Johannesburg. Then he was appointed to serve as a curate at a church near Benoni, an industrial town east of Johannesburg. (A curate is an assistant clergyman who helps more senior priests with services and parishioners.) Tutu undertook his duties at St. Alban's Church in Daveyton, one of Benoni's black townships. The only accommodation available for Tutu, his wife, Leah, and their three children was a garage not far from the church. Tutu called the garage "our main bedroom, the children's bedroom, our lounge and dining room all rolled into one."[10] A curtain divided the garage in two; the family used the smaller, second room as a kitchen. The Tutus had to exist in these cramped and unhealthy conditions for the next year. They weren't the only ones living in poor conditions in Daveyton, however. The township had few trees and little vegetation; most houses had dirt yards. Many of the residents of this gritty, urban landscape worked in the factories on the East Rand, as the urban area east of Johannesburg was called. At St. Alban's, Tutu helped with baptisms, marriages, funerals, and Sunday school. He also delivered his first sermons there. He preached in a variety of languages, including Sotho, Xhosa, Zulu, and English.

After a year as a curate in Daveyton, Tutu was formally ordained as a priest in late 1961. His first assignment as a full-fledged priest was in Thokoza, the black township in Alberton, southeast of Johannesburg. Tutu was put in charge of a new church in Thokoza. He had more autonomy now, and his family could enjoy the relative comfort of a small, four-room house. Tutu developed a deep compassion for his flock in Thokoza. Most of the members of his congregation were overwhelmingly poor and devoutly religious. He made regular visits to his parishioners' homes and listened intently to their joys and concerns. He was impressed by their piety and humbled by the trust they placed in such a young and inexperienced priest. Despite the difficult conditions apartheid imposed on his parishioners, Tutu found the priesthood deeply rewarding. Soon he would have the opportunity to enhance his qualifications as a priest thousands of miles from home.

NOTES

1. Naomi Tutu, "Introduction" in *The Words of Desmond Tutu* (New York: Newmarket Press, 1989), pp. 18–19.

2. Shirley du Boulay, *Tutu: Voice of the Voiceless* (Grand Rapids, MI: William B. Eerdmans, 1988), p. 46.

3. Mmutlanyane Stanley Mogoba, "From Munsieville to Oslo," in *Hammering Swords Into Ploughshares: Essays in Honor of Archbishop Mpilo Desmond Tutu*, ed. Buti Tlhagale and Itumeleng Mosala (Grand Rapids, MI: William B. Eerdmans, 1987), p. 25.

4. Alan Paton, *Apartheid and the Archbishop: The Life and Times of Geoffrey Clayton* (New York: Charles Scribner's Sons, 1973), p. 277.

5. Mothobi Mutloatse, "Mutloatse on Tutu," *Ecunews* 8 (December 1984): p. 17.

6. Du Boulay, *Tutu*, p. 49.

7. Mutloatse, "Mutloatse on Tutu," p. 17.

8. Philip Frankel, *An Ordinary Atrocity: Sharpeville and Its Massacre* (New Haven: Yale University Press, 2001), p. 50.

9. Frankel, *An Ordinary Atrocity*, p. 183.

10. Mutloatse, "Mutloatse on Tutu," p. 17.

Chapter 5

RELOCATING TO BRITAIN

In 1962, a new set of doors opened for Tutu. He was encouraged to enroll at King's College at the University of London to begin studying for a degree in theology. The principal of St. Peter's, Father Aelred Stubbs, hoped to groom Tutu for a teaching position at his institution and urged his former student to bolster his academic credentials. Tutu liked the idea, applied to King's College, and was accepted. Thanks largely to the backing of Father Stubbs, he received scholarships from the Anglican diocese of Johannesburg and the Community of the Resurrection. He also received financial assistance from the World Council of Churches and King's College itself. But the South African government was less than enthusiastic about Tutu's plans. Officials were reluctant to let Tutu leave South Africa because of their deep-rooted suspicions toward black South Africans who had been educated overseas. In their view, these black South Africans sometimes returned home with dangerous ideas of freedom and racial equality. Despite their concerns, the South African government issued Tutu with a passport and allowed him to travel.

Tutu arrived in Britain in September 1962 and was soon joined by Leah and his two eldest children, Trevor and Theresa. Naomi, the Tutus' youngest child, initially remained behind with a grandmother in Johannesburg. The Tutus moved into a two-bedroom apartment near a park in north London. In exchange for these lodgings, Tutu worked on Sundays at St. Alban's Church in the wealthy suburb of Golder's Green. The Tutus would spend the next three years in London while Desmond studied for a bachelor's degree in divinity at King's College. Living and studying in Britain would turn out to be one of the most important experiences of Desmond Tutu's life.

Life in Britain had improved significantly since the end of the Second World War. More consumer goods were available, such as refrigerators, televisions, and cars. Standards for housing were rising. More students received the opportunity to study at universities. In general, the British people enjoyed greater social mobility than ever before. But Britain was not as powerful as it had been before World War II. By the early 1960s, its empire had been mostly dismantled, and its rate of economic growth was slower than that of other leading industrialized nations, such as West Germany, Japan, and the United States. Although most British citizens considered themselves to be at least somewhat religious, only a minority attended church regularly. British society had grown more secular, and the Church of England, though still one of the country's most important institutions, did not have quite the same influence it once did.[1]

Britain was gradually becoming a multiracial society in the 1950s and '60s. In those two decades, immigrants from India, Pakistan, and the former British colonies in the West Indies arrived in increasing numbers. A small number of African immigrants entered Britain as well in this era. Some Britons were uncomfortable with the influx of so many different racial groups into their country. The British government enacted various immigration controls in the 1960s but also passed laws prohibiting discrimination against legal immigrants. Even with the surge in immigration from Asia, Africa, and the Caribbean, Britain was still an overwhelmingly white society by the time the Tutus arrived in 1962.

Although it took Desmond and Leah time to get used to the British weather, they fell in love with the country, especially the freedom and dignity it offered them. "It was marvelous," Desmond recalled. "We didn't have to carry our passes anymore and we did not have to look around to see if we could use that bath or that exit."[2] Tutu felt his humanity was being restored after so many years living as a third-class citizen in South Africa. He found the freedom of speech in Britain especially exhilarating. Speakers' Corner in Hyde Park attracted outspoken people who sometimes voiced outlandish views. No matter how controversial their beliefs, they could speak their mind without fear of arrest. In fact, the police were there to protect the speakers' right to free speech, not harass them. The contrast with South Africa could hardly have been more striking. And unlike in South Africa, government leaders in Britain regularly faced stiff questioning from journalists.

Tutu felt liberated in this new environment. Living in Britain, he would later say, helped him "to become more fully human."[3] Two anecdotes illustrate this point. Once Tutu was standing in line at a British bank when a white man suddenly cut in front of him. The teller told the man that he would have to wait his turn because Tutu was there first. Tutu could hardly believe his ears. He was not used to being accorded such respect, respect that was routinely denied to black South Africans back home.[4] He later recalled another aspect of life in Britain:

> When we walked about in London, if we saw a policeman we would cross the road to ask him the way, even if we knew where we were going, just for the pleasure of being called "Sir" and "Madam." In South Africa we would have been asked for our passes and run the risk of getting arrested.[5]

The sociopolitical climate in Britain was not the only thing that Tutu found stimulating; he also immersed himself in the academic world at King's College at the University of London. King's College specialized in theological education and provided Tutu with a tolerant and challenging environment in which to study. His degree program was designed to train him as a "traditional Anglican theologian."[6] Tutu took courses in the Old Testament and the history and philosophy of religion. He also studied Hebrew, enhancing his considerable skills as a linguist. He already knew Afrikaans, English, Greek, Sotho, Tswana, Venda, Xhosa, and Zulu. His tutors were so impressed with his academic performance that they encouraged him to embark on the honor's course in divinity, which he did.

While in Britain, Tutu was exposed to a predominantly white community for the first time. He had never served a white congregation before, but this was his task at St. Alban's Church in Golder's Green. He became intimately acquainted with this congregation and soon had more sustained contact with whites than he had ever had in South Africa. To his surprise, he discovered that the desires and problems of his white parishioners were no different from those of blacks. Looking back on his stay in Britain in the early 1960s, Tutu said, "I was ministering for the first time on a regular basis to white people as a priest. I don't know what I was expecting but it turned out that they were human beings with the ordinary strengths and foibles, resentments and triumphs, as well as the sins of ordinary human beings."[7] Tutu worked with the resident priest at St. Alban's and quickly built a close relationship with the church's members.

Even though he was thousands of miles from his own country, Tutu began to feel at home in Britain because he was surrounded by his family and made many new friends. He had a support network at St. Alban's and King's College and had friends who took him to social events and cricket matches. He also renewed his ties with fellow South Africans in London whenever he could. At one point he participated in a conference on nationalism at which Oliver Tambo and Ambrose Reeves spoke. Tambo, a fellow black South African graduate of St. Peter's, led the ANC's overseas operations in the early 1960s. Tutu was also reunited with his beloved mentor Trevor Huddleston, who had been recalled to Britain in 1957 because the Community of the Resurrection feared that he would be arrested in South Africa.

Being in Britain helped Tutu dispel any bitterness he might have felt toward whites because of his experiences under apartheid. His stay also helped him jettison any feelings of inferiority he might have had toward whites. He developed the confidence to disagree with whites "openly" and "vigorously" for the first time and overcame the habit of automatically deferring to whites. He felt freer to express his opinions than he ever had back home. Tutu would draw upon this newfound confidence during his later career in South Africa. He would say things that other black South Africans would shy away from because many had internalized a sense of racial inferiority after so many years of segregation and apartheid.[8]

As Tutu's confidence grew in Britain, so did his family. Desmond and Leah's fourth child, a daughter they named Mpho, was born in 1963. She would spend the first three years of her life in England and grew up with an unmistakably English accent. The Tutus' third child, Naomi, joined the family in Britain during the same year that Mpho was born. While Desmond studied at King's College, Leah looked after the children and did most of the shopping, cooking, cleaning, and laundry for the family. Having been trained as both a teacher and a nurse, she missed working outside the home and hoped to draw upon her professional skills again in the future. Desmond was a part-time curate and thus did not earn much money, but the family did manage to go on short holidays together.

Tutu earned his Bachelor of Divinity degree with honors in 1965. At the graduation ceremony at London's Royal Albert Hall, the Queen Mother awarded the degrees in her capacity as chancellor of the University of London. Tutu had originally planned to return to South Africa after receiving his bachelor's degree, but he became interested in continuing his studies in Britain at the graduate level. In an October 1964 letter to the dean of King's College, Tutu explained his interest in staying on for a graduate degree: "Please, I hope it does not sound big-headed or, worse, downright silly. But if I go back home as highly qualified as you can make me, the more ridiculous our Government's policy will appear to earnest and intelligent people."[9]

His logic was persuasive. Tutu's scholarships were extended for another year so that he could continue to study and support his family in Britain.

He decided to focus on Islam for his master's degree at King's College. Before he left South Africa, he had written an essay on Islam that was awarded the prestigious Archbishop's Essay prize. Concentrating on Islam for his master's degree would enable him to expand his knowledge of this all-important religion in Africa and the wider world.

As Tutu began his master's program, he and his family moved to a parish in Bletchingley, Surrey, south of London. Bletchingley's population reflected Britain's class divisions to a greater extent than did Golder's Green. Some members of the Bletchingley parish were aristocratic landowners who lived in manor houses; others were working-class people who lived in subsidized housing. Tutu took up residence at St. Mary the Virgin Church in Bletchingley, where he was the first black curate that that congregation had ever had. He became completely dedicated to serving his new parishioners. He helped raise the congregation's consciousness about South Africa's racial problems but refrained from making his sermons overtly political. He was not afraid to speak out on other issues he felt strongly about, whether regarding practices for communion or the conduct of his parishioners. He also encouraged the parish to work with local Catholics and Methodists whenever it could to foster an ecumenical tradition. During his year at St. Mary's, Tutu took regularly scheduled retreats to read, pray, and meditate. But he was not one to cloister himself in his study. In fact, Tutu was sometimes spotted traveling around his parish in a motorcycle.

The people at St. Mary's embraced Tutu. They loved his sense of humor and were delighted by his warmth and exuberance. After a midnight mass at Christmas, some of Tutu's parishioners looked on in wonder as Tutu "danced in the starlight" outside, spontaneously expressing his joy over the occasion.[10] Tutu's experiences in Bletchingley—and in Britain in general—convinced him that blacks and whites could live together in harmony and enrich each other's lives, even if they had yet to do so in his own country.

Desmond was not the only one in his family to enjoy life in Bletchingley. His family had more space (a house) and income than they had had in London. The children seemed especially well adjusted, despite being the only four black children in town. Trevor attended a private school where he did very well. The Tutus' family life was certainly progressing differently than it would have had they remained in South Africa. For example, Desmond and Leah wanted to give their children more freedom to express themselves than they had had as children growing up in South Africa. They had been taught to be quite meek in the presence of adults and not to make eye contact with their elders. But Britain was a more per-

missive society than South Africa, particularly in the 1960s. During that
decade, new measures were passed that overturned tradition: the British
government abolished the death penalty, decriminalized homosexuality,
liberalized abortion laws, and lifted restrictions on theatrical perform-
ances and public entertainment.[11] The more liberated environment of
Britain convinced the Tutus to give their own children more leeway. But
sometimes being a less authoritarian parent could try Desmond's patience.
He recalled,

> I remember saying to our youngest, who was then a very chirpy
> three year old, and quite sure that there were very few things
> that she did not know in the world: "Mpho, darling, please
> keep quiet, you talk too much!" Do you think she was at all de-
> flated by this rebuke? Not at all—quick as a shot she retorted:
> "Daddy, you talk a lot too. You talk all by yourself in church!"[12]

Desmond and Leah had been taught not to talk back to adults, but they
encouraged their children to be less inhibited. They didn't want to per-
petuate the authoritarianism of South Africa while they were in Britain—
or, for that matter, when they returned home. Even though Desmond and
Leah were not as strict as their parents had been, they did insist on high
standards and discipline. Pandering to their children's every whim was out
of the question, because this would prevent them from growing up into responsible adults.

After nearly four years in Britain, Tutu earned his Master's of Theology
degree from King's College in 1966. He and his family now had to say
goodbye to their friends in Bletchingley and return home. A farewell
party was held in their honor, attended by parishioners from St. Mary's
and people in the community at large. The partygoers showered the Tutus
with going-away presents, including a car that the family could use in
South Africa. Strong personal bonds had obviously developed between
the Tutus and the community, and the farewell was a tearful occasion.
Friends from St. Mary's were overwhelmed with sadness both because
they would miss Desmond and because they recognized the difficulties
awaiting the Tutus back in South Africa. Apartheid, after all, was still
alive and well.

NOTES

1. Walter L. Arnstein, *Britain Yesterday and Today: 1830 to the Present*, 8th ed.
(Boston: Houghton Mifflin, 2001), pp. 398–404.

2. Judith Bentley, *Archbishop Tutu of South Africa* (Hillside, NJ: Enslow, 1988), p. 44.

3. Quoted in Mothobi Mutloatse, "Mutloatse on Tutu," *Ecunews* 8 (December 1984): p. 17.

4. David Winner, *Desmond Tutu*, People Who Helped the World Series (Harrisburg, PA: Morehouse, 1989), p. 24.

5. Desmond Tutu, *The Essential Desmond Tutu*, comp. John Allen (Cape Town: David Philip, 1997), p. 34.

6. Shirley du Boulay, *Tutu: Voice of the Voiceless* (Grand Rapids, MI: William B. Eerdmans, 1988), p. 61.

7. Mutloatse, "Mutloatse on Tutu," p. 17.

8. Du Boulay, *Tutu*, p. 60 and Joseph Lelyveld, "South Africa's Bishop Tutu," *New York Times Magazine*, 14 March 1982, p. 44.

9. Quoted in Du Boulay, *Tutu*, p. 62.

10. Quoted in Du Boulay, *Tutu*, p. 68.

11. Peter Dorey, *British Politics Since 1945* (Cambridge, MA: Blackwell, 1995), pp. 102–108.

12. Desmond Tutu, *Crying in the Wilderness: The Struggle for Justice in South Africa* (Grand Rapids, MI: William B. Eerdmans, 1990), p. 93.

Chapter 6

RETURN TO SOUTHERN AFRICA

On his way back to South Africa from Britain in 1966, Tutu spent two months in Jerusalem to study Islam, the subject of the master's program he had just completed. He was shocked by the degree of tension he encountered between Arabs and Israelis. To a large extent, his experiences in the Middle East foreshadowed the racial tensions he would confront back home.

South Africa had experienced a period of unprecedented repression while Tutu and his family lived in Britain. In the early 1960s, the main antiapartheid groups had been banned; detention without trial expanded; and the torture of political prisoners increased. The military wings of the ANC and the PAC had been effectively neutralized; most militants were either in jail, killed, or in exile. The most prominent black South African political leader in the early 1960s was Nelson Mandela. After he was arrested in 1962, Mandela and his colleagues were put on trial for sabotage the next year. Mandela used the trial to tell the court and the wider world why he felt obligated to fight against an unjust form of government. Despite his eloquence, he and his seven comrades were found guilty by a white judge and sentenced to life in prison in 1964. Had the government not been concerned about international opinion, Mandela and his colleagues would probably have been executed.

The South African government limited freedom of expression in the 1960s by censoring or banning books, magazines, music, and films that it deemed objectionable or subversive. The government controlled radio service in the country and refrained from introducing television until 1976. Some newspapers did have the freedom to publish articles or editorials that were relatively critical of the government, but when publishers or editors feared provoking the government's wrath, they often censored themselves. Elections for whites were held at regular intervals, but the National Party only seemed to gain support with each election. South Africa was clearly moving in the opposite direction from the rest of Africa in the 1960s. In most of the continent, Africans were gaining their independence from European colonial rule; in South Africa, white rule became stronger.

A major platform of Prime Minister Hendrik Verwoerd's government was to offer limited rights to black South Africans in ethnically based territories known as "homelands." This policy envisioned Africans as citizens of small ethnic states within South Africa, not as citizens of South Africa itself. Although Verwoerd labeled his policy "separate development" or "separate freedoms," the homelands were clearly part of his government's divide-and-rule strategy toward the black South African majority. Most homelands were fragmented pieces of territory whose combined area amounted to approximately 13 percent of South Africa's landmass. They could never accommodate the aspirations of 75 percent of South Africa's people. The homelands quickly became overcrowded territories with few economic opportunities. Many black South Africans had never set foot in the homelands to which they were assigned by the government. Between the 1960s and the 1980s, millions of black South Africans who lived on land that the government rezoned for another racial group were forcibly removed from their homes in South Africa proper and sent to live in remote homelands. Prime Minister Verwoerd envisioned that these homelands would one day become independent states, administered by Africans who chose to collaborate with the South African government. Once they were established, some African-run homelands were more brutal than the South African government in rooting out opposition. Some corrupt African civil servants viewed employment in the homeland governments as a way to enrich themselves. Not surprisingly, the homelands policy was never accepted by most black South Africans—or the outside world.

The Verwoerd era came to a sudden and violent end in 1966, when the prime minister was assassinated by a mixed-race messenger who stabbed him in Parliament. Verwoerd was succeeded by B. J. Vorster, the minister of justice in the previous administration. Vorster had been interned in South Africa during the Second World War for sympathizing with the Nazis. While serving under Verwoerd, he had greatly expanded the power of the South African security police, which adopted the fitting acronym, BOSS, short for the Bureau of State Security. Vorster authorized increased surveillance of suspected government opponents, expanded detention without trial, and created an environment in which police were free to torture suspects, even if it meant killing them in the process. As prime minister, Vorster was not as adamant about maintaining segregation in all public places (such as hotels, restaurants, and cinemas) as Verwoerd had been, but he was committed to ensuring that white minority rule would continue indefinitely, no matter what the cost.

Tutu arrived back in South Africa around the time that Vorster became prime minister. He and his family faced a difficult readjustment upon their return to the Johannesburg area. Tutu wrote a British friend about having to ask for permission from white officials to visit his parents, having to carry a pass, and having to avoid whites-only entrances. Exposing his children to life under apartheid was heartbreaking. Once when the family was having a picnic at a beach in East London (Cape province), the Tutus' youngest daughter, Mpho, wanted to play on the swings. But because the swings were on the whites-only part of the beach, Desmond had to tell his child no. He felt terribly diminished, just as his father had probably felt when he was stopped for his pass when Desmond was a boy. Desmond could not shield his children from South African realities. When they inevitably encountered racism, he urged them not to be nasty back, even if they were treated discourteously. Never believe you are inferior to anyone, he told them. When driving their children to school in Swaziland, a country on South Africa's eastern border, the Tutus were confronted with a series of difficulties. Few public restrooms were open to black South Africans, and many restaurants along the way only served blacks at the back door, if at all. After experiencing freedom in Britain, the Tutus found it hard to accept third-class treatment in their own country. It took all of Tutu's Christian compassion to avoid becoming embittered.

The Tutus soon moved to the small town of Alice in the eastern Cape so that Desmond could begin teaching at the Federal Theological Seminary. They arrived in Alice in 1967 and would remain there for the next three years. The Federal Theological Seminary, known as Fed Sem, educated African ministers for service in the Anglican, Congregational, Methodist, and Presbyterian churches. Black South African students had studied theology at the South African Native College (also in Alice) since 1920, but after the government took over the college in 1959, the main English-speaking churches established Fed Sem a year later. St. Peter's Theological College, the site of Tutu's early theological training, moved from the Johannesburg area to Fed Sem in the early 1960s. There it became known as St. Peter's Anglican College. Each denomination at

Fed Sem had its own college, principal, and staff; the denominations shared the assembly hall, administration building, and library. The institution trained black ministers only; white clergymen received their training elsewhere.

When Tutu arrived at Fed Sem, the institution was headed by Father Aelred Stubbs, who had been principal of the old St. Peter's Theological College in Johannesburg when Tutu was a student there. Stubbs had helped arrange Tutu's admission to the University of London, raised scholarship funds for him, and finally hired him to teach at Fed Sem. Although the seminary's students were black and most of the instructors were white, the races mixed surprisingly freely, as if apartheid did not exist. Because of the relatively open environment there, Fed Sem was an ideal place for Tutu to readjust to South Africa after his stay in Britain. He quickly made friends with the students and staff and relaunched his teaching career. He and Simon Gqubule were the only two Africans on the teaching staff at Fed Sem in 1967. Tutu taught church doctrine and Greek. He sought to both expand his students' knowledge and help them grow spiritually. He also taught his students "how to approach theology in the black South African context."[1] Tutu required his students to work hard and assigned texts by pioneering theologians. He didn't want his students to be second class to anyone intellectually, as blacks were often considered to be by both white South Africans and themselves.

Tutu also wanted to keep his own mind sharp. While teaching at Fed Sem, he enrolled in the PhD program in theology at the University of South Africa (UNISA), hoping to focus on Moses and the Koran. His growing political involvement eventually prevented him from completing his doctorate, but this was not due to any lack of ability on his part.[2]

Although their initial readjustment to South Africa had been difficult, the Tutus liked living in Alice. The Community of the Resurrection gave them a nice house where they regularly entertained friends and students. The Tutus' three oldest children were enrolled at private schools in Swaziland; their youngest child, Mpho, stayed with Desmond and Leah in Alice. Expressing the family's overall contentment, Leah wrote, "The Seminary is a marvelous place. The friendliness and cooperation is such that you would have to travel the far corners of the Republic and still be lucky if you found anything like it."[3]

Besides being a lecturer at Fed Sem, Tutu also became the Anglican chaplain at Fort Hare, the famous university for Africans in Alice. First known as the South African Native College, Fort Hare had been established by the Church of Scotland in 1916 and was the only university open to black South Africans in the early twentieth century. Nelson Mandela and Oliver Tambo had attended Fort Hare; previous African professors there included D. D. T. Jabavu and Z. K. Matthews, distinguished members of the black South African intelligentsia.

The apartheid era brought sweeping changes to Fort Hare. In 1959, the South African government seized control of the university and turned it into an institution for Xhosa-speaking students only. This was part of the government's plan to stress ethnic differences among Africans whenever possible. The university, like most other educational institutions for blacks, would be run by the Bantu education department. In the late 1960s, the atmosphere at Fort Hare was less relaxed than that at Fed Sem. The seminary was friendly and encouraged intellectual freedom and inquiry, while the environment at Fort Hare seemed more oppressive. According to Tutu, the university students would often come to Fed Sem to seek "refuge when trouble erupted at Fort Hare."[4]

The university was located in a part of South Africa that had a rich tradition of African resistance to white rule. In the late 1960s, it became one of the leading centers of a new political movement just as Tutu became chaplain—black consciousness. Students in the forefront of this movement believed that black South Africans needed to regain the initiative in the fight against apartheid and not rely on their white liberal allies. They sought to break away from these allies and develop their own leaders and ideas. They believed that blacks needed to fight apartheid in their own organizations, build up their self-esteem, and liberate themselves psychologically from feelings of inferiority. Part of the inspiration for the black consciousness movement in South Africa came from the black power movement then gaining momentum in the United States. "Black man, you are on your own" became the black consciousness movement's rallying cry. The new emphasis on black initiative differed from the "nonracial" approach of the 1950s, when many leading antiapartheid activists stressed that like-minded people of all races should work together for freedom in South Africa. The black consciousness movement soon spread rapidly among black South African students. It filled the void created in the wake of the banning of the ANC and the PAC earlier in the decade. The most famous black consciousness leader was Steve Biko, a young black medical student at the University of Natal in the late 1960s whose story was later dramatized in the film *Cry, Freedom* (1987).

Being chaplain at Fort Hare put Tutu in the thick of the emerging black consciousness movement. Many of the university's students actively supported the new movement. Tutu agreed that black students needed to

reaffirm their own dignity as a race, but his experiences in Britain had
made him optimistic about the potential for cooperation between black
and white allies. He had embraced the principle of nonracialism, which
de-emphasized racial differences among people. Tutu was not viewed as a
"radical" by his students, but he was still respected by black consciousness
activists. He too agreed that apartheid was immoral, and he was not shy
about saying so. During a sermon he gave at Fort Hare in 1968, Tutu com-
pared the citizens of Czechoslovakia with black South Africans, since
both were victims of government repression. This was a risky thing to say,
given that Fort Hare was under the control of the apartheid government.
After the sermon, Tutu was never invited to preach at the university
again.

There were growing signs that after the intimidation and repression of
the early sixties, black South African students were becoming bolder. Part
of this had to do with the black consciousness movement. Trouble began
at Fort Hare in 1968 shortly after the appointment of a new rector, J. J. de
Wet. When students met with de Wet to discuss student-administration
relations, they received a chilly reception. In the second half of the 1968
academic year, Fort Hare students began to boycott classes to protest the
university administration's policies. The students called for better education, the hiring of more qualified staff, and the departure of the deputy
minister of Bantu education when he visited the campus. Despite their
protests, de Wet refused to meet with the students' elected leaders. Then
500 of the university's 550 students occupied the lawn in front of the administration building during a nonviolent sit-in. In response, de Wet ordered that banners and graffiti be removed from campus and that the
students end their protest. He threatened them with disciplinary action if
they did not comply. When students ignored de Wet's ultimatum, he
called in the police to break up the demonstration. They arrived with
dogs and tear gas and surrounded the students at gunpoint. Tutu rushed to
the university from his office at Fed Sem to offer his support to the students, but police tried to stop him when he sought to speak to some of the
protesters. Tutu made it clear that if the students were arrested, he would
have to be arrested as well. Despite his pleas, the police forced the students to their rooms to pack and then put them on buses for the train station so that they could return home. Tutu remained with the students
during the standoff, greatly impressing the protesters, black consciousness
leaders included. "It was a deeply moving experience," one student leader
remembered. "The students flocked around him in relief and excitement,
asking for his blessing."[5] There was little Tutu could do but offer them his

blessing. All student strikers were suspended from the university and 22 were expelled. The students' treatment at the hands of the administration and the police distressed Tutu so much that he wept the next day at mass.[6]

After three years in Alice, Tutu was about to be promoted to vice principal of Fed Sem. It was widely believed that he might even become principal one day. But in 1970, he was invited to become a lecturer in theology at the University of Botswana, Lesotho, and Swaziland (UBLS) in Roma, Lesotho. The job in Lesotho offered Tutu a higher salary, which would help him pay his children's private school tuition. Living in Lesotho would also put him closer to Swaziland, where his two eldest children could continue to study at private schools. The two youngest children, Naomi and Mpho, could attend school on the campus of UBLS, thus saving the family money. Tutu accepted the offer and moved his family beyond South Africa's borders once again.

Lesotho, known as the "mountain kingdom" for its jagged peaks and high elevation, is entirely surrounded by South Africa. It had been the home of the southern Sotho people since the early nineteenth century. In 1868, Chief Moshoeshoe convinced the British to declare his kingdom a protectorate. Following Chief Moshoeshoe's death in 1870, the monarchy continued throughout the twentieth century, although its powers were limited. The territory was known as Basutoland before independence and was eventually given a separate administration from other southern African colonies that had more overtly white supremacist governments. Many of the country's men went to work in the South African gold mines. When Lesotho gained its independence from Britain in 1966, it was very poor and economically dependent on South Africa. In the years immediately following independence, the Lesotho government stayed on friendly terms with the giant neighbor that surrounded it.

The university that hired Tutu had been established in 1945 by the Roman Catholic Church and was originally known as Pius XII Catholic University College. Students from all over Africa came to study there for degrees initially awarded by UNISA. In 1964, the governments of Botswana, Lesotho, and Swaziland took financial responsibility for the university and assumed administrative control. The university became secular and independent from that point onward; its key function was to train civil servants, teachers, and lawyers. In 1966, the institution became known as the University of Botswana, Lesotho, and Swaziland.

Tutu began teaching at the university in 1970, just a few years after Lesotho gained its independence from Britain. Tutu immediately took a liking to the mountainous country, for both its landscape and its freedom from apartheid. When he was not teaching, he enjoyed riding horseback to visit mountainside chapels. The political environment of Lesotho was not as tranquil as Tutu would have liked, however. The South African government had a network of informers there, and the government and the opposition party were divided along religious lines (Catholic versus Protestant). By the time Tutu assumed his post in Lesotho, he was already being monitored by the South African government, which deemed him potentially subversive.[7]

During his three years in Alice, Tutu had thought deeply about how the Christian churches should react to apartheid. Some of his work involved serving on commissions that focused on Christian responsibilities in apartheid society. When Tutu arrived in Lesotho, "black theology" was spreading in southern Africa. This theology catered to the victims of racial oppression, whether in South Africa or elsewhere. Tutu began to immerse himself in black theology at UBLS and make his own original contributions to it.

Tutu was immediately attracted to black theology. He believed it would help blacks regain their pride and dignity, which had been eroded by years of discrimination. They needed to be reassured that they were children of God, just like whites. Black theology reminded blacks that God was on the side of the oppressed. Tutu drew parallels between the oppression facing black South Africans and that experienced by the Israelites in the Bible. Eventually the oppressed reach the promised land, with God's help. As Tutu wrote, "[God] sides with the poor, the hungry, the oppressed, the victims of injustice."[8] Tutu also noted how the sense of inferiority among black South Africans dehumanized them and caused them to treat each other poorly. Once they emerged from self-loathing, he believed, the oppressed must leave bitterness behind. Like his mentors from the Community of the Resurrection, Tutu was convinced that true Christians needed to establish God's kingdom on Earth, not retreat from the problems of the world. Christians in South Africa had a responsibility to expose the inhumanity of apartheid and work to end oppression. In his view, Christians of all races needed to speak for the weak and the meek, to expose evil and seek to end it.

As a proponent of black theology, Tutu wanted to communicate his perspective to a wider audience, not just other theologians or his students. He used sermons and speeches, not densely worded academic texts, to spread his message whenever he could. Some black South Africans had begun questioning the relevance of Christianity in their lives because so many white Christians supported apartheid. Tutu, on the other hand, believed that Christianity could be a religion of liberation.

NOTES

1. Siqibo Dwane, "Archbishop Desmond Tutu—A Personal Tribute," in *Hammering Swords Into Ploughshares: Essays in Honor of Archbishop Mpilo Desmond Tutu*, ed. Buti Tlhagale and Itumeleng Mosala (Grand Rapids, MI: William B. Eerdmans, 1987), p. 19.

2. Shirley du Boulay, *Tutu: Voice of the Voiceless* (Grand Rapids, MI: William B. Eerdmans, 1988), p. 74.

3. Quoted in du Boulay, *Tutu*, p. 72.

4. Quoted in Mothobi Mutloatse, "Mutloatse on Tutu," *Ecunews* 8 (December 1984): p. 17.

5. Du Boulay, *Tutu*, p. 79.

6. Dwane, "Archbishop Desmond Tutu," p. 20.

7. Du Boulay, *Tutu*, p. 83.

8. Du Boulay, *Tutu*, p. 86.

Chapter 7

SECOND STAY IN BRITAIN

A new opportunity materialized for Tutu in late 1971, while he was still teaching at the University of Botswana, Lesotho, and Swaziland. Walter Cason, the acting director of the London-based Theological Education Fund, asked Tutu to consider an appointment as one of the fund's associate directors. Tutu agreed to put his name forward. The dean of King's College at the University of London wrote a letter of recommendation for Tutu. He believed his former student would do a good job but worried that the position would take Tutu away from southern Africa, where he was greatly needed. In the end, Tutu was offered the job and accepted, despite having been at UBLS only two years. He knew his family would be happy to return to Britain and believed that his children's education would benefit from the move.

The Theological Education Fund (TEF) was a branch of the World Council of Churches (WCC), which had been founded in Amsterdam in 1948. The WCC originated as a movement to encourage unity and cooperation among Christian churches. It sought to promote ecumenical fellowship, service, and study and was destined to grow into a huge international organization. Eventually the WCC brought together more than 300 churches and denominations in over 100 countries. It represented 400 million Christians in Orthodox, Protestant, and independent churches. (The Roman Catholic Church was not a member of the WCC, but it cooperated with the council in many areas.) Although headquartered in Geneva, Switzerland, the WCC had a global reach. The English-speaking churches in South Africa were founding members of the WCC in 1948, as were the Dutch Reformed Church synods in the Cape and

Transvaal provinces. The council thus linked South African Christians with Christians in the wider world.

When Tutu accepted the job at TEF, the WCC was viewed with great hostility by the South African government. The reason was simple: ever since its founding, the WCC had declared racial segregation to be contrary to the gospel. In expressing its concern over racial segregation, the WCC reflected a worldwide Christian concern over apartheid that grew over time. At a WCC-sponsored conference in Johannesburg nine months after the Sharpeville tragedy of 1960, participants drafted a statement criticizing the apartheid policy and proclaiming that equal rights should be enjoyed by all. Not surprisingly, the conference infuriated the South African government. It so angered leaders of the Dutch Reformed Church in South Africa that they withdrew their denomination from the WCC in protest. The WCC continued to generate controversy in the years to come. In 1966, the council held a conference on church and society at its Geneva headquarters. During the conference, delegates discussed the extent to which Christians should support revolutionary struggles in the world. In later meetings in South Africa, antiapartheid theologians discussed the relevance of the conference for their own country.

The church-state conflict in South Africa escalated in 1968. In that year, the South African Council of Churches sponsored a commission that published "A Message to the People of South Africa." The message declared that apartheid was unchristian because it made fellowship among people of different races all but impossible. The document was sent to all English and Afrikaans ministers and immediately became widely publicized—and controversial. While some English-language newspapers and ministers expressed support for the message, Afrikaans newspapers condemned it. Prime Minister Vorster exploded. In a speech just weeks after the message's publication, Vorster threatened dire consequences for those "who wish to disrupt order in South Africa under the cloak of religion." He warned that it would be unacceptable for clerics to "do the kind of thing here in South Africa that Martin Luther King did in America" and told the clergy to "cut it out, cut it out immediately for the cloak you carry will not protect you if you try to do this in South Africa."[1] The firestorm surrounding the message showed that when it came to apartheid, church and state were on a collision course in South Africa.

Tensions rose even further in 1970, when the WCC launched its Program to Combat Racism. Under this program, the WCC's executive committee decided to offer financial support to liberation movements fighting white minority governments in southern Africa [South Africa, Rhodesia,

South-West Africa (now Namibia), Angola, and Mozambique]. The council gave money to the ANC and the PAC for medical supplies and supported families of jailed antiapartheid leaders. Although WCC leaders resolved only to give humanitarian aid—not weapons—to the liberation movements, their decision created an uproar in South Africa. Most white South Africans were irate. They viewed the WCC as supporting communists and terrorists and urged their denominations to withdraw from the WCC. Prime Minister Vorster was equally adamant. He announced that if the South African member churches did not sever their connection to the council, they would face unspecified penalties. Leaders of South Africa's English-speaking churches found themselves in a dilemma. They had not been briefed about the Program to Combat Racism in advance, nor did they formally endorse it. But they tended to support most aspects of the program, except the portion that committed the WCC to assisting liberation organizations that engaged in violence. In the end, the WCC's South African member churches all stayed in the organization but criticized the council for appearing to endorse violence by granting aid to armed liberation movements. The South African government was not satisfied. It henceforth prohibited any South African funds from being sent to the WCC and banned council representatives from visiting South Africa for the next 21 years.

It was against this background that Tutu accepted a job with the Theological Education Fund, a branch of the WCC. When he applied to the South African government for permission to travel to Britain to take up the position, authorities initially refused to grant him a passport. The government had regarded him with suspicion ever since he supported student protesters as the Anglican chaplain at Fort Hare in 1968. The government's growing antagonism toward the WCC did not help matters. Tutu decided to appeal the government's decision by writing to Prime Minister Vorster. In his letter, Tutu said it was in South Africa's best interest that he be allowed to go to Britain because there he could channel educational funds to the country. His position as associate director of TEF would also lend prestige to South Africa. After receiving Tutu's letter, Vorster relented and instructed government officials to grant Tutu a passport.[2] It would be one of the few times that Vorster was swayed by Tutu's reasoning.

Desmond, Leah, and their four children arrived in London in January 1972. Conditions in Britain in the 1970s were unsettled, though not unstable. The country faced rising inflation, a worsening problem in Northern Ireland, more militant trade unions, and growing concerns over immigration. Britain received an influx of immigrants in 1972, when the

Ugandan dictator Idi Amin expelled Asians from his country. The British government allowed these Asians to settle in the United Kingdom if they had British passports. Twenty-eight thousand immigrants decided to accept the offer, stoking anti-immigration sentiments in some quarters. The Tutus generally received a warm welcome. The one glaring exception occurred when a stranger mistook Tutu for a Ugandan and snapped, "You bastard, get back to Uganda."[3] Luckily such treatment was extraordinarily rare.

Desmond and his family moved into a house in Grove Park, a suburb in southeastern London popular with commuters. Besides having a nature reserve, Grove Park's other claim to fame was that it had been home to Edith Nesbit (1858–1924), the author of the beloved novel *The Railway Children*. The Tutus would live in their home on Chinbrook Road for three years, a fact noted with pride by city officials and historians after Desmond became world famous.[4] Tutu's office at the Theological Education Fund was in Bromley, just south of Grove Park. Bromley was also important in the literary world, for it was the birthplace of author H. G. Wells (1866–1946). The Tutus very much enjoyed being back in Britain. The four children were enrolled in good schools and thus experienced another reprieve from Bantu education. The family felt totally comfortable as black South Africans in Britain. Far from being plagued by feelings of inferiority, they all grew in self-confidence during their second extended stay in England. The contrasts with South Africa continued to amaze them. Despite being a foreigner, Leah was often canvassed by various British political parties around election time. The irony was that she didn't even have the right to vote in her own country. Desmond had long recognized the value of experiencing life outside South Africa. As he said later, "I know … just how living in free societies has helped my family and me develop into slightly better human beings, released from the claustrophobia of apartheid. Consequently, I am almost obsessed with the concern that as many South Africans, especially blacks, get the opportunity to experience what it means to be accepted and treated as a human being."[5]

Not all African residents of Britain felt as liberated as the Tutus. For example, the Nigerian author Buchi Emecheta struggled for years with poverty and prejudice after she moved to Britain in the 1960s.[6] But because they were escaping apartheid, the Tutus' euphoria over living in Britain was understandable. They felt grateful to be free, even if this freedom was only temporary. They also had a steady source of income, a two-parent household, and a built-in social network due to their ties to the Christian church.

While working at TEF, Tutu also served as honorary curate at St. Augustine's Church in Bromley. He participated in services whenever he could and enjoyed a warm relationship with the parishioners, just as he had in Golder's Green and Bletchingley in the 1960s. As the vicar of St. Augustine's recalled years later about Tutu, "It was always as though the very place was lit up by his presence and permeated by his infectious laughter."[7] Tutu always made time for reflection, prayer, and reading, no matter how hectic his schedule was. Quiet times with God nourished his spirit. He urged his parishioners and coworkers in Britain to nurture their relationship with God as well.

Naturally, most of Tutu's time in London was spent working for the Theological Education Fund. TEF had been established in 1958 to support theological education in Asia, Africa, and Latin America. It was an ecumenical organization from the start, just like its parent organization, the WCC. The original funding for TEF came from American missionaries and a grant from John D. Rockefeller Jr., the famous American philanthropist whose family made their fortune in the U.S. oil industry. Part of TEF's work in the 1970s involved studying ways that theological education could be contextualized or modified in the Third World to reflect local conditions and traditions. Tutu supported this effort. The associate directors of TEF came from the areas for which they were responsible: Tutu was from Africa, while his colleagues represented Asia, South America, and North America. Tutu liked working in an office with so many different nationalities because it helped open his eyes to perspectives and problems of the rest of the world.

As director of TEF's programs in Africa, Tutu assessed requests for funding and presented his findings at TEF's annual meetings. He was committed to raising money for theological education in Africa. To do so, he had to learn how to be both an administrator and a fundraiser. Developing skills in these areas would work to his advantage during his later career in South Africa. Tutu's colleagues at TEF found him both outgoing and sensitive. Although he could be offended by careless language and discourteous behavior, he and his coworkers adjusted to each other's idiosyncrasies and formed a cohesive team. Tutu's secretary once told a visitor that her South African boss was the best fundraiser TEF had ever had.[8]

Travel was an important part of Tutu's job. He took several trips to Africa each year between 1972 and 1975 and spent nearly half of each year investigating theological education programs on the continent. Many of his trips took him to unstable or crisis-ridden areas. He traveled to Uganda when it was under the iron-fisted rule of Idi Amin; Ethiopia just before the overthrow of Emperor Haile Selassie; and Nigeria after the

Biafran War. In Nigeria, he witnessed the immense suffering and disloca-
tion that the war had inflicted on Africa's most populous country. Tutu
also spent time in Zaire, the vast central African country under the dictatorship of Mobutu Sese Seko. African authorities sometimes regarded
Tutu with suspicion. At Uganda's Kampala airport, security police detained and searched him. He was also searched by police at the airport in
Salisbury, Rhodesia. Officials in both countries suspected that Tutu was
carrying material critical of their governments. While Tutu was in fact a
critic of both regimes, he was allowed to proceed in both instances without being arrested. Tutu hoped South Africa could avoid some of the social and political problems he saw in the rest of Africa, but the continent
did not leave him in despair. He was especially impressed at how Africans
ran their own churches. Even though he frequently met people speaking
different languages during his travels in Africa, he often felt a strong
Christian fellowship with those he encountered. He also did not hesitate
to speak out against the situation in South Africa during his travels. He
was so outspoken, in fact, that some wondered whether he would be allowed back into South Africa in the future.

Although Tutu had developed pride in black accomplishments and in
his own black identity, he experienced some pangs of doubt during a trip
to Nigeria. Shortly after boarding a plane in that country, he noticed that
both the pilot and the copilot were black. He began to shift in his seat un-
comfortably. Recalling the incident, he said, "I had a nagging worry about
whether we were going to make it. Could these blacks fly this plane without a white person at the controls? Whether you are aware of it or not,
somewhere inside of you, you had always been aware of white people at
the controls."[9] Of course Tutu arrived at his destination intact. He also
traveled to Asia during his time at TEF. Such extensive travel experiences
were highly unusual for a black South African and gave him an excep-
tionally broad view of the world and its problems. His new international
perspectives led him to become more politically engaged than ever before.

Within a few years of Tutu's hiring at TEF, some speculated that he
might become the organization's next director. But Anglican leaders in
South Africa had their eyes on Tutu as well. In 1974, the position of
bishop of Johannesburg became vacant and Tutu's old mentor at St.
Peter's, Father Stubbs, nominated Tutu for the position. Instead, the elective assembly selected Timothy Bavin, the dean of Johannesburg, as
bishop. Then Bavin asked Tutu to replace him as dean.

These developments posed a dilemma for the Tutus. Leah had happily
readjusted to life in Britain and was not eager to leave. The Tutus' three

daughters were attending good schools, and son Trevor had enrolled at Imperial College in London. Desmond was not sure what to do. Like his wife, he was content in England and did not want to disrupt his family's life or break his contract with TEF, which required him to serve for three more years. But he knew that some South Africans wanted him to return home. Many friends and colleagues told him that South Africa needed someone of his stature and education to point the way forward for Christians in the country. They said he needed to serve as an example, to inspire others, and to lead. After taking time to reflect during a spiritual retreat, Tutu made his decision. He would return to South Africa and assume the position in Johannesburg. Despite enjoying life in Britain, Tutu's children supported his decision because they too believed that their father was needed back home. Leah eventually agreed as well. Once officials at TEF released Tutu from his contract, he prepared to become the first black Anglican dean of Johannesburg. His days as an anonymous black clergyman were about to come to an end.

NOTES

1. John W. de Gruchy, *The Church Struggle in South Africa* (Grand Rapids, MI: William B. Eerdmans, 1986), p. 118.

2. Curt Schleier, "Desmond Mpilo Tutu," *Investor's Business Daily*, 3 April 2001.

3. Shirley du Boulay, *Tutu: Voice of the Voiceless* (Grand Rapids, MI: William B. Eerdmans, 1988), p. 91.

4. Lewisham Online: Local history, Grove Park, www.lewisham.gov.uk/Local History/ historygrovepark.asp.

5. Mothobi Mutloatse, "Mutloatse on Tutu," *Ecunews* 8 (December 1984): p. 17.

6. See Buchi Emecheta, *Second Class Citizen* (New York: George Braziller, 1974) and *Head Above Water* (Portsmouth, NH: Heinemann, 1994).

7. Du Boulay, *Tutu*, p. 93.

8. T. S. N. Gqubule, "They Hate Him Without a Cause," in *Hammering Swords Into Ploughshares: Essays in Honor of Archbishop Mpilo Desmond Tutu*, ed. Buti Tlhagale and Itumeleng Mosala (Grand Rapids, MI: William B. Eerdmans, 1987), p. 38.

9. Judith Bentley, *Archbishop Tutu of South Africa* (Hillside, NJ: Enslow, 1988), p. 50.

In a township east of Johannesburg, Archbishop Desmond Tutu wades into an angry crowd of blacks who had doused a police informer with gasoline, July 10, 1985. (AP/WIDE WORLD PHOTOS)

Former South African President P. W. Botha (left) shakes hands with Truth Commission chairman Tutu, November 21, 1996. (AP/WIDE WORLD PHOTOS)

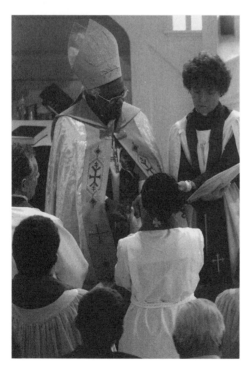

Mpho Tutu (kneeling) is ordained by her father, the archbishop, in Christ Church in Alexandria, Virginia, January 17, 2004. (AP/WIDE WORLD PHOTOS)

Chapter 8

NEW CHALLENGES IN SOUTHERN AFRICA

Apartheid was still in full force when Tutu returned to South Africa in 1975. Prime Minister Vorster had authorized the removal of some whites-only signs at a handful of restaurants and hotels, but black South Africans still faced pass laws, Bantu education, limited job and housing options, and many discriminatory laws and attitudes. And they still could not vote in the land of their birth. The homelands policy had actually gained momentum. In 1970, the government passed the Bantu Homelands Citizen Act. This law stripped blacks of their South African citizenship and assigned them citizenship in a homeland according to their ethnic group. They were only allowed to stay in urban areas in "white" South Africa on a temporary basis if they met certain conditions. Furthermore, those temporary residence rights could be revoked at any time. Each year thousands of blacks were forced to leave their homes in white areas and move to the homelands. Building upon Hendrik Verwoerd's dream, Vorster planned to treat the homelands as "independent" countries within South Africa. The first homeland to be granted such independence was the Transkei in 1976.

After a period of relative calm in the mid- to late 1960s, there were signs of renewed protest on South Africa's horizon. Strikes in Durban in 1973 signaled that workers were becoming more militant. The philosophy of black consciousness had spread widely. And South Africa was more isolated internationally than ever before. The country was banned from competing in the Olympic Games and many other world sporting competitions. Criticism of apartheid from the United Nations and the Organization of African Unity had escalated. The independence of Angola and

Mozambique from Portuguese control in 1975 boosted the confidence of those who wanted to see majority rule in South Africa.

Once he returned to South Africa in 1975 to assume the position of dean of Johannesburg, Tutu would be in the spotlight for the first time in his life. His appointment marked the beginning of his transition from private citizen to public figure. It would be something he would have to get used to for the rest of his life. When he became the first black dean of Johannesburg, he also became the highest-ranking black Anglican in South African history. The position of dean of Johannesburg was one of the highest in the Anglican Church hierarchy in South Africa, behind only the archbishop of Cape Town, the dean of the province, and the bishop of Johannesburg. No wonder that a crowd of 3,000 people attended Tutu's installation, including prominent South African Christian leaders of many faiths.

Anglican officials invited the Tutus to live in the dean's residence in Houghton, one of Johannesburg's wealthiest white suburbs. But the Tutus broke with tradition and chose to live in Soweto instead, the huge black township southwest of Johannesburg. Not eager to be considered "honorary whites," they also did not want to be isolated from the poverty facing black South Africans. The family soon moved into a house in the Orlando West section of Soweto. The two eldest children, Trevor and Theresa, stayed in Britain to continue their studies; the two youngest, Naomi and Mpho, enrolled in school in Swaziland. Leah began working at the South African Institute of Race Relations, where she focused on the conditions facing domestic workers. Such workers, employed by most white South African families, often faced low pay, long hours, and few legal protections.

The Tutus' new home in Soweto was approximately 12 miles from central Johannesburg. The largest urban black settlement in South Africa, Soweto sprawled over 50 square miles and was home to more than a million residents. The first African township in what would become Soweto had been established in the early 1900s. The population surged as more black migrants streamed into the area seeking work. A whole network of settlements was developed in the area, since blacks were restricted from living in most of Johannesburg itself. The greatest population influx occurred in the 1950s and '60s. In 1963, the separate townships south of Johannesburg were collectively named Soweto, an acronym for South Western Townships. By the 1970s, Soweto encompassed 28 separate townships. The area was governed by the West Rand Administration Board, an arm of the National Party government.

The government wanted inhabitants of Soweto to feel like temporary visitors, not permanent urban dwellers, so they invested as little as possible in the township. Although some middle-class blacks lived in Soweto and there were a few nice neighborhoods with large homes, most of the massive township was dusty, monotonous, crime ridden, and lacking in basic services. Residents could not own their own homes; instead, they paid rent to the government board that administered Soweto. The only areas in which black South Africans could exercise full citizenship rights were the homelands. Most homes in Soweto were small, virtually identical brick dwellings with iron roofs and two to four rooms. The typical house was about the size of "the average living room in a white middle class home."[1] By the mid-1970s, only 25 percent of Soweto houses had running water; most residents had to get their water from communal taps outdoors. Only 15 percent of Soweto homes had electricity. Often a cloud of smoky haze hung over the township, generated by thousands of coal stoves burning simultaneously. Very few households had telephones. In 1976, Soweto had 39 public telephones, one for every 26,000 people. There were few shops and businesses in Soweto and few lights to illuminate the dusty and unpaved streets at night. Alcoholism and crime were serious problems in the area. In fact, Soweto had one of the highest murder rates in South Africa. Gangsters known as "tsotsis" roamed the streets and terrified residents, especially at night and on payday. According to a 1975 newspaper survey, Soweto residents yearned for the right to own their own homes, more schools, better street lighting, better transportation, more telephones, better roads, and more shops and recreational facilities.[2]

Most white South Africans never saw what life was like in Soweto or any other black township. The government actively discouraged whites from seeing how their black fellow citizens lived. A sign at one of Soweto's main entry points read, "Non-Bantu entering this area must have a permit."[3]

Every morning Tutu commuted from Soweto to downtown Johannesburg, where his office at St Mary's Cathedral was located. In addition to his responsibilities as dean of the Johannesburg diocese, Tutu also served as rector (clergyman in charge) of St. Mary's. It was a multiracial church, which made it relatively unique in South Africa. Tutu had visited the cathedral even before he became a priest to reflect in the quiet atmosphere of one of the chapels. He loved hearing the boy choristers rehearse and seeing their angelic faces, knowing that they "could be up to all kinds of mischief."[4] Besides enjoying the music emanating from the cathedral,

Tutu liked the fact that people could enter the building to escape the noise of the city and pray in a quiet, peaceful place.

Despite South Africa's divided society, St. Mary's brought together people of all races to worship. Both Tutu's staff and the congregation were racially diverse, as were the choir, servers, and ministers. This gave Tutu hope that perhaps South Africa was changing for the better. "There was just nothing more impressive than when St. Mary's was full to overflowing with all God's children of all races," Tutu wrote, "with the long procession of catechists, sub-deacons and clergy winding their way slowly into a cathedral packed to the rafters." When he knelt in the dean's stall at St. Mary's during high mass and saw blacks and whites worshipping together, tears of joy sometimes streamed down his cheeks.[5] He believed that such multiracial services broke down apartheid's barriers, just as God intended. He also liked how black and white children at St. Mary's would play and pray together, presenting a model for what South African society could become.

Racial tensions were not altogether absent from St. Mary's. Some white parishioners left the church when Tutu became rector, hurting him deeply. Those who stayed were sometimes taken aback by Tutu's actions. For example, some objected when he announced a sudden change in liturgy to what had been a relatively conservative congregation. Tutu also announced his support for the ordination of women and replaced masculine pronouns in services with more gender-neutral terms. He broadened the language to include the whole world, not just South Africa. Some colleagues and parishioners embraced the new perspectives, while others felt uncomfortable. At one point Tutu wanted St. Mary's to finance a bus to go to Soweto, pick up black worshippers, and bring them to St. Mary's. Some members of the congregation questioned this initiative and charged Tutu with being careless with the parish's budget. On the other hand, many black members of the congregation welcomed the changes Tutu introduced. Their new dean had brought them into the mainstream of the church for the first time and invited them to help make decisions. Never had they felt more at home or more valued as members of the congregation. Tutu sought to affirm the dignity of his black parishioners and challenge his white parishioners to become less materialistic and more sensitive to the needs of the downtrodden.

Tutu knew that he was more visible as dean of Johannesburg than he had ever been before. He sought to use his leadership position as a platform to speak out against injustice. He believed that the time had come for him to play a political role in South Africa, to show that politics and theology could not be separated. Some Christians in South Africa—and elsewhere—believed that religion should focus on purely spiritual matters and not concern itself with the world. Proponents of this view believed that the church should not question the social order in which it existed. Others believed that the church should have a direct bearing on society by working for justice. Tutu took the latter position, as did his former mentors Trevor Huddleston and Aelred Stubbs. Father Stubbs in particular encouraged Tutu to become more politically engaged when he took up the deanship. Tutu viewed politics and religion as a "seamless garment." From his perspective, it was inconceivable that God cared only about what happened on Sunday, not the rest of the week. It was inconceivable that "He does not much care about the plight of the hungry, the dispossessed, the voiceless, the powerless, that He does not take sides." For Tutu, being neutral when faced with injustice was to accept injustice.[6]

In an effort to further his political education, Tutu met with black consciousness leaders such as Mamphela Ramphele and community leaders in Soweto such as Nthato Motlana. Talking with these leaders and other less prominent individuals raised his awareness about the conditions and struggles facing the black community. In the speeches and sermons he gave as dean, Tutu urged his fellow South Africans to recognize the humanity of others, regardless of their race. He insisted that reconciliation was only possible between equals. "The freedom of the white man is bound up with that of the black man," he wrote in 1975. "So long as the black man is dehumanized and unfree, so long too will the white man remain dehumanized and unfree because he will be plagued by fear and anxiety."[7] While Tutu was hopeful that South Africa's problems could be resolved peacefully, he worried that the patience of black South Africans might eventually evaporate. In a letter to a British friend, Tutu expressed his fear that black South African youth were becoming increasingly bitter and alienated. He worried that they would become a lost generation if they weren't given reasons to hope. His sentiments turned out to be prophetic.

Tutu sensed the growing anger among Soweto youth in early 1976. While on a three-day spiritual retreat in Johannesburg in May, Tutu felt moved by God to write a letter of warning to Prime Minister Vorster. His May 6 letter was direct but respectful. He wrote that like the Afrikaners, black South Africans yearned for freedom and dignity in the land of their birth. While the removal of some whites-only signs was encouraging, it was not sufficient. "Blacks are grateful for all that has been done for them," Tutu wrote, "but now they claim an inalienable right to do things for themselves, in cooperation with their fellow South Africans of all races." He told the prime minister, "I write to you, Sir, because like you, I am deeply committed to real reconciliation with justice for all, and to peaceful change to a more just and open South African society in which the wonderful riches and wealth of our country will be shared more equitably."

Tutu emphasized that white South Africans would continue to feel insecure until their black fellow citizens were free. "We need one another and blacks have tried to assure whites that they don't want to drive them into the sea." He continued, "I am writing to you, Sir, because I have a growing nightmarish fear that unless something drastic is done very soon then bloodshed and violence are going to happen in South Africa almost inevitably.... A people made desperate by despair, injustice and oppression will use desperate means. I am frightened, dreadfully frightened that we may soon reach a point of no return." Tutu explained that he had seen the consequences of violence during his travels in the Middle East, Africa, and Northern Ireland and that neither he nor other black South Africans wanted such violence in South Africa. "We blacks are exceedingly patient and peace-loving," he wrote.

Tutu realized that Vorster couldn't abolish apartheid overnight, so he asked the prime minister to show his commitment to peaceful change by taking three steps: (1) granting urban blacks permanent citizenship rights in South Africa, (2) repealing the pass laws, and (3) holding a national convention open to all South African leaders to discuss the evolution of South Africa into a more just society. According to Tutu, only these bold steps could prevent the situation in South Africa from deteriorating rapidly. He closed his letter by quoting a prayer that was spoken during Friday services for justice and reconciliation at St. Mary's Cathedral. It read, in part,

> O Lord, make us instruments of Thy peace
> Where there is hatred, let us sow love
> Where there is injury, pardon
> Where there is despair, hope
> Where there is darkness, light
> Where there is sadness, joy[8]

Vorster wrote back three weeks later, accusing Tutu of engaging in political propaganda. He refused to take any of the steps Tutu recommended.

Tutu's warnings about growing black disillusionment were frighteningly accurate. The black consciousness movement had spread to Soweto schools by the mid-1970s, emboldening students to question the acquiescence of the older generation and to resist apartheid more forcefully. Conditions in Soweto schools contributed to the rising tide of discontent. Not only was Bantu education still in place, but there were not enough class-rooms, desks, equipment, or qualified teachers to meet student demand. In the mid-1970s, the government spent about 15 times more money for the education of each white child than it did for each black child. Edu-cation for whites was free and compulsory; education for blacks was nei-ther.

Tensions rose in early 1976 after the government required that Afrikaans be used as a medium of instruction at Soweto high schools. Stu-dents would have to learn half of their subjects in Afrikaans, including math, history, and biology. Parents, teachers, and students believed the policy was implemented so that black South Africans could more readily understand orders from their Afrikaner bosses. Not only was Afrikaans perceived as the language of the oppressor, but few black teachers or stu-dents in Soweto were fluent in the language. This made teaching and learning not only distasteful, but all but impossible. Students clearly pre-ferred to be taught in English, but when they and their teachers voiced their initial opposition to the Afrikaans policy, the government ignored them. Students then began to pressure their teachers to stop teaching in Afrikaans. Later they refused to take exams and burned Afrikaans books and test papers. On May 17, 1976, some students began to boycott classes to protest the Afrikaans policy. Prominent newspaper editor Percy Qoboza and antiapartheid member of Parliament Helen Suzman urged the minister of Bantu education to rescind the policy, but their pleas were ignored as well.

Government officials seriously underestimated the simmering resent-ment in Soweto. That May, the white chairman of the West Rand Ad-ministration Board (WRAB) told a newspaper that "the broad masses of Soweto are perfectly content, perfectly happy. Black-white relationships at present are as healthy as they can be. There is no danger whatever of a blow-up in Soweto."[9] That pronouncement would prove to be a colossal misjudgment.

On the morning of June 16, 1976, less than six weeks after Tutu's warn-ing to Prime Minister Vorster, approximately 15,000 Soweto students congregated in Orlando West to begin a protest march. Most were be-tween 10 and 20 years old. They carried homemade signs reading, "To hell with Afrikaans" and "If we must do Afrikaans, Vorster must do Zulu." Po-lice quickly confronted the students near Orlando West High School in Tutu's own neighborhood. They ordered the students to disperse, and when this failed, they released dogs into the crowd and fired tear gas. Stu-dents reacted by throwing stones. The police then opened fire, killing 12-

year-old Hector Petersen in the process. Sam Nzima's photograph of another youth carrying the boy's lifeless body became the most famous image
in South African history. After this initial confrontation, violence
erupted all over Soweto. Students set fire to government buildings and vehicles and killed two white WRAB officials. Police reinforcements arrived and sealed off the township. As clouds of black smoke rose, violence
continued throughout the afternoon and evening, claiming the lives of
more Soweto students. Tutu's dire predictions had come true.

At the time of the unrest, Tutu was the top Anglican clergyman in the
Johannesburg area because his superior, Bishop Bavin, was abroad. Tutu
was in his office at St. Mary's Cathedral in central Johannesburg on the
morning of the 16th when someone telephoned him to say that Soweto
school children were being shot. When Tutu called the police department
for more information, police representatives were uncooperative. He finally got through to a brigadier and identified himself, but the officer
hung up on him. He then rushed to Soweto to assess conditions and console parents and children. Just days after the unrest, the government
banned all public meetings in Soweto, but mass funerals were held despite
the ban. Tutu told mourners at one such funeral, "We are getting sick and
tired of trying to tell the Prime Minister that the present South African
way of life is unholy and oppressive."[10] He spoke about the struggle at vig-
ils in Soweto in the days ahead, offering comfort and inspiration whenever he could. On the first Sunday after June 16, Tutu told his mostly
white congregation at St. Mary's, "We have been really shattered by the
deafening silence from the white community. You will say, what could we
do? And all I would say to you is, what would you have done had they
been white children? And that is all we would have wanted you to have
done."[11]

By June 23, at least 176 people had been killed in the Soweto unrest,
most of whom were young black students. Many more had been seriously
injured. Unrest then spread to other townships in the Johannesburg region; by August, even townships in Cape Town, almost 1,000 miles away,
were plagued by violent protests. The death toll nationwide rose to over
500 by early 1977. The government eventually rescinded its Afrikaans
policy and announced that schools could choose their own medium of instruction, but this was little comfort to those who had lost loved ones in
the violence. An uneasy calm returned to Soweto by 1978.

The Soweto protests of 1976 represented the worst racial unrest in
South Africa since the advent of apartheid in 1948. On the one hand, the
tragic events showed the length to which the South African government
was willing to go to crush dissent. On the other, the disturbances illus-

trated the new determination of young black South Africans to resist apartheid, no matter what the cost. Following the unrest, waves of young Sowetans fled South Africa and went into exile to join the ANC or the PAC, thus reenergizing the liberation movement. The violence focused international attention on apartheid in South Africa to an even greater extent than had the Sharpeville massacre 16 years earlier. Unlike the period after 1960, dissent was not completely crushed after 1976.

When the crisis in Soweto erupted, Tutu was preparing to become bishop of Lesotho, a post he had agreed to assume even before he wrote Prime Minister Vorster in May. Tutu was eager to rise in the church hierarchy, but when he was first being considered for the position in Lesotho, he felt great inner turmoil. His work as dean of Johannesburg was important, and he felt that his relationship with the congregation at St. Mary's was beginning to gel. He expressed his reservations about becoming bishop, but church leaders from Lesotho sent a delegation to Soweto in an effort to change his mind. Even though Tutu secretly hoped that someone else would be chosen, he was elected bishop of Lesotho. He felt obligated to accept.

Tutu was consecrated as bishop of Lesotho on July 11, 1976, at a ceremony at St. Mary's Cathedral in Johannesburg. He had served as dean of Johannesburg for less than a year, much to the regret of his old mentor Father Stubbs. Some at St. Mary's accused Tutu of using their parish merely as a stepping stone to a higher position. Tutu wept when it came time to leave South Africa because he knew the country was in the midst of a crisis. Still, he believed his new appointment was God's wish. In August 1976, Tutu was enthroned at St. James's Cathedral in Maseru, the capital of Lesotho. Among those attending his installation were Lesotho King Moshoeshoe II, Queen Mamohato, and Prime Minister Chief Leabua Jonathan. Tutu was now the mountain kingdom's highest-ranking Anglican clergyman.

Chief Jonathan had been in power since 1965. When he lost the 1970 election, he nullified the vote and remained in office. His government's executive branch was not balanced by a strong legislature or court system, but opposition political parties did exist and criticism of the government was allowed. King Moshoeshoe II's power was purely ceremonial. Lesotho's government, while authoritarian, was not a dictatorship like Mobutu's in Zaire or Idi Amin's in Uganda. Chief Jonathan had begun to adopt a more confrontational stance toward South Africa in the early 1970s. He hoped that criticizing apartheid would win Lesotho allies in the outside world. As a result of his policy, relations between Lesotho and South Africa deteriorated. In June 1976, Lesotho broke off talks with South Africa on a joint hydroelectric project when the Soweto uprising occurred. In November 1976, the African-American Institute held a conference in Maseru. Among those attending were key opponents of apartheid, including Andrew Young, soon to become the American ambassador to the UN; Senator Dick Clark; Percy Qoboza, editor of the Soweto-based *World* newspaper; and representatives from the ANC and PAC. In January 1977, South Africa withdrew its grain subsidy for Lesotho in retaliation for Lesotho's increasing willingness to criticize apartheid.

Despite its hostility toward apartheid, Chief Jonathan's government became more economically dependent on South Africa in the 1970s. Thousands of Lesotho's citizens still depended on migrant labor in South Africa for their income. Agriculture in Lesotho was stagnant, partly because so many of the country's residents sought higher wages in South Africa. Lesotho imported much of its food from South Africa and purchased all of its electricity from South Africa's power grid. Partly because of this dependence, the Lesotho government did not openly give refuge to South Africa freedom fighters in the period immediately following the Soweto unrest.[12]

Despite his traumatic departure from South Africa, Tutu felt at home in Lesotho. Between 80 and 90 percent of Lesotho's people were Christian, mostly Roman Catholic, Evangelical, or Anglican. Tutu liked the rituals associated with the church—the pageantry, the vestments, and the ceremonies. But he didn't want people to see him as exalted or unapproachable. He didn't want to be addressed as "My Lord" in the way that some bishops were. He urged all visitors to come to the front door of his residence, not the back. During his tenure as bishop, he participated in services at many different churches, took communion to the sick and the elderly, and visited prisoners. Forty priests reported to him. He could have delegated less-senior priests to visit remote parishes, but he wanted as much personal contact with his flock as possible. Sometimes Tutu flew to outlying parishes, but other times he could only get to his destination on horseback. He commented on one particularly memorable horseback ride in a letter to friends in December 1976: "There was no rapport between me and the horse—when I go up, he goes down with rather unpleasant consequences for certain unmentionable parts of my anatomy."[13] Some of his journeys on horseback lasted eight hours. Tutu grew to love the Basotho people. Just as he had felt at home in the Western environment of Britain, he also embraced the African environment of Lesotho. He particularly liked African food, hymns, and styles of worship.

Tutu was still intent on stressing the links between church and society, whether he was in South Africa or not. He didn't hesitate to criticize the government of Lesotho when he felt its actions were questionable. "Injustice is injustice, whoever...perpetrates it," he wrote.[14] The Lesotho government reacted by occasionally criticizing him in public.

After Tutu had been in Lesotho for just over a year, another tragedy struck the land of his birth—the death of black consciousness leader Steve Biko. Biko had been the movement's best-known leader since it emerged among black South African university students in the late 1960s. Although Tutu had never met Biko, he endorsed many of the young leader's philosophies. Thousands of other South Africans did so as well. Biko even impressed a number of international visitors who came to see him at his home in King William's Town in the eastern Cape in the 1970s. But the South African government viewed Biko as a major threat. Authorities banned him and put him under surveillance for most of the 1970s. (A "banned" person could not write for publication, be quoted, attend public gatherings, or meet with more than one person at a time.) While on his way to a political meeting on August 18, 1977, Biko was stopped at a roadblock near Grahamstown and taken into police custody. He was brought to security police headquarters in Port Elizabeth, brutally assaulted during interrogation, and eventually lapsed into a coma. In early September, police loaded Biko into a police van naked and in chains and drove him to a police hospital in Pretoria, more than 700 miles away. He died on September 12, 1977, three months short of his 31st birthday. News of Biko's tragic death made headlines all over the country and sparked an outpouring of grief both in South Africa and abroad. Just 15 months after Soweto erupted, South Africa faced yet another tragedy.

Tutu was asked to give the eulogy at Biko's funeral. Thirty thousand mourners arrived at the massive outdoor service in King William's Town on September 25, 1977. It was one of the most highly charged, emotional funerals in South African history. Although the police prevented some black South Africans from going to the funeral, throngs of black and white mourners did manage to attend, as did representatives of foreign governments, including the United States. In his eulogy, Tutu urged the mourners to realize that injustice in South Africa had dehumanized whites as well as blacks. He asked the crowd to pray for white South African leaders and policemen because they needed to regain their humanity, as did their victims. Plagued by anguish himself, Tutu continued,

> It all seems such a senseless waste of a wonderfully gifted person, struck down in the bloom of youth. What can be the purpose of such wanton destruction? God, do you really love us? Oh, God, how long can we go on appealing for a more just or-

dering of society where we all, black and white together, count
not because of some accident of birth or biological irrelevance,
where all of us count because we are human persons created in
your own image?

Tutu then drew a parallel between Biko's death and the crucifixion of
Jesus. After the latter event, he said, it seemed as if the powers of evil had
overwhelmed the Earth. But with Christ's resurrection, "life has tri-
umphed over death. Life and goodness and love reign forevermore, over
hatred and evil and darkness. We too, like the disciples of Jesus, have been
stunned by the death of another man in his thirties. A young man completely dedicated to the pursuit of justice and righteousness, of peace and
reconciliation." Tutu believed that Biko had been called by God to re-
mind blacks that they were people of intrinsic value. But, revealing as
much about himself as the man he eulogized, he continued, "Steve knew
and believed fervently that being pro-black was not the same thing as
being anti-white."

Tutu pleaded with authorities to listen to the cries of the people before
the country slid over the precipice. "Nothing will stop people once they
are determined to achieve their freedom," he insisted. He assured the
mourners that victory over oppression was around the corner, despite the
darkness that seemed to envelop their lovely land. "We thank and praise
God for giving us such a magnificent gift in Steve Biko," he said. "Let us
dedicate ourselves anew to the struggle for the liberation of our beloved
land. Let us all, black and white together, not be filled with despondency
and despair. Let us blacks not be filled with hatred and bitterness. For all
of us, black and white together, shall overcome, nay indeed we have already overcome."[15] In the emotional atmosphere of Biko's funeral, a
leader less committed to reconciliation could have made a bitter, anti-
white speech. But like Biko, Tutu stressed that whites were not the enemy,
the system of apartheid was. Tutu's message was one of hope, not hatred.
Because God sided with the oppressed, they would ultimately triumph.

Such hope did not seem particularly well founded at the time. On October 19, 1977, the South African government embarked on a massive security crackdown. It banned black consciousness organizations and jailed
the movement's key leaders; banned the *World*, the country's most widely
read black newspaper, and detained its editor Percy Qoboza; banned antiapartheid theologian Beyers Naudé, an Afrikaner; and banned *Daily Dis-
patch* editor and Biko confidante Donald Woods. Although Tutu strove to
sound hopeful in public, privately he could not help but worry about the
future of his "beloved land."

Tutu was destined to return to South Africa sooner than he thought. During his first year as bishop of Lesotho, he was asked to become the general secretary of the South African Council of Churches. He had expected to stay in Lesotho for at least five years. When he sought advice from Anglican officials, they encouraged him to accept the new post. At the time, Tutu's wife, Leah, was national director of the Domestic Workers and Employers Project. This organization advocated better conditions and pay for South Africa's domestic workers. Trevor was still studying in London, while Theresa had begun medical school in Botswana. Naomi and Mpho were still attending school in Swaziland. Tutu decided to begin the new job in early 1978. He knew his place was in South Africa, where he could minister directly to those struggling for freedom. Some Anglicans in Lesotho were angry that Tutu was leaving after such a short stay; others accepted his new appointment more gracefully, believing that he needed to play a role in South Africa. At least Tutu had prepared a Lesotho priest to take over as bishop for him. Father Stubbs was convinced that Tutu's destiny lay in South Africa and that God himself had paved the way for his return.

NOTES

1. Philip Bonner and Lauren Segal, *Soweto: A History* (Cape Town: Maskew Miller Longman, 1998), p. 18.

2. Patricia Farrow, *Soweto: The Complete Township Guide* (Johannesburg: Soweto Spaza, 1997), p. 33.

3. Farrow, *Soweto*, p. 3.

4. Desmond Tutu, *Hope and Suffering* (Grand Rapids, MI: William B. Eerdmans, 1984), p. 133.

5. Tutu, *Hope and Suffering*, pp. 134–35.

6. Tutu, *Hope and Suffering*, pp. 36–39.

7. Shirley du Boulay, *Tutu: Voice of the Voiceless* (Grand Rapids, MI: William B. Eerdmans, 1988), pp. 100–101.

8. Desmond Tutu, *The Rainbow People of God: The Making of a Peaceful Revolution*, ed. John Allen (New York: Doubleday, 1994), pp. 6–13.

9. Bonner and Segal, *Soweto*, p. 77.

10. Bonner and Segal, *Soweto*, p. 90.

11. Du Boulay, *Tutu*, p. 107.

12. Richard Weisfelder, "Lesotho: Changing Patterns of Dependence," in *Southern Africa: The Continuing Crisis*, ed. Gwendolen M. Carter and Patrick O'Meara (Bloomington: Indiana University Press, 1979), pp. 249–68.

13. Du Boulay, *Tutu*, p. 111.

14. Du Boulay, *Tutu*, p. 117.

15. Tutu, *The Rainbow People of God*, pp. 16–21.

Chapter 9

GENERAL SECRETARY OF THE SOUTH AFRICAN COUNCIL OF CHURCHES

During Tutu's tenure as bishop of Lesotho, South Africa's young blacks had become more determined than ever to resist apartheid. But many whites still had a false sense of security. A new South African prime minister, P. W. Botha, took office in 1978 and believed that white South Africans needed to accept reforms to apartheid in order to remain in control. In his words, they had to "adapt or die."[1] He quickly demonstrated his own willingness to undertake reforms. His government recognized the right of blacks to reside permanently in urban areas, recognized black trade unions, authorized improvements in black townships, eased segregation of public areas, relaxed job reservation laws, and spent more on black education. By moving away from the rigid apartheid of the past, Botha raised black South African expectations considerably.

But Botha feared that if he went too far, he would lose the support of Afrikaner hard-liners. His fear of a right-wing backlash slowed his reforms, especially in the 1980s. The key elements of apartheid remained intact—the Group Areas Act, forced removals, population registration, the pass laws (until 1986), and the repression of dissent. There were no plans to give blacks equal voting rights. The government still assigned blacks citizenship in the homelands and prepared to grant "independence" to more of these territories in the 1980s. Prime Minister Botha also sought to destabilize South Africa's neighbors so that they would be unable to mount a serious challenge to white minority rule in South Africa. Botha's policies eventually triggered strong opposition from conservative whites, who opposed reform in general, as well as black students, trade unions, and many church leaders, who believed that Botha's reforms

didn't go far enough. One of the most vigorous critics of Botha's government was the South African Council of Churches (SACC).

The SACC had originated as the Christian Council of South Africa in
1936. Its members included most English-speaking churches, except the
Baptist Church. Some African independent churches became affiliated
with the Christian Council as well; the Catholic Church was an observer,
not a member. The Dutch Reformed Church was originally a member, but
it withdrew because of the Christian Council's criticisms of apartheid. At
a 1949 conference, the council declared that apartheid was divisive and
harmful to South Africa. It called for a wider franchise, better education,
and more job opportunities for all. In 1968 the Christian Council
changed its name to the South African Council of Churches. Its relationship with the government soured shortly thereafter. When the SACC declared apartheid to be contrary to the gospel, Prime Minister Vorster
warned churches not to meddle in politics. The SACC replied that as
long as the government declared apartheid to be consistent with Christianity, churches were obligated to speak out. Even before Tutu's assump-
tion of the SACC leadership, the council had condemned the role of the
South African military in defending apartheid and called conscientious
objection to military service a valid Christian option. It consistently
called for nonviolent change in South Africa. Furious at the SACC's defiance, the government secretly organized the Christian League in the
mid-1970s to counteract the council's influence.

Tutu became general secretary of the SACC in March 1978, six
months before P. W. Botha became South Africa's new prime minister.
Tutu was the first black ever to head the SACC. He assumed the leadership at a tense time, just following the government's crackdown of October 1977. Because the antiapartheid Christian Institute and most black
consciousness organizations had been banned, the SACC was one of the
few vehicles left to articulate black aspirations. The stage was set for Tutu
to play an important leadership role in South Africa. He was determined
to make the SACC one of South Africa's most visible human rights organizations. In so doing, both he and the council would become lightning
rods for the government's wrath.

When Tutu took over, the SACC had 20 member churches, 4 observer
churches, and represented almost 15 million Christians. The council's
primary purpose was to "present a common Christian stand on major social issues."[2] One branch of the SACC supported theological education
programs; another supported humanitarian projects (health, welfare,
jobs); and another dealt with social activism (legal aid, investment, support for prisoners' families). Tutu faced a daunting administrative task

upon assuming the SACC leadership. The council was composed of 16 divisions, published several periodicals, and had an annual budget of four million rand ($4.6 million). It had grown so large that it had become distant from some of its affiliates and hard to manage. Tutu was intent on keeping the disparate affiliates united. He helped coordinate the work of different departments, determined priorities, and administered funds. He also helped restructure the SACC to ensure that its departments cooperated more fully.

Fundraising took up much of Tutu's time. Member churches did not donate consistently, and money from the private sector was scarce, so Tutu had to solicit funds constantly. He was particularly successful in encouraging donations from overseas. Besides raising money, Tutu also spent it. One of the SACC's key funds was the Asingeni Fund, originally established to aid families who lost loved ones during the 1976 unrest. The portion of the fund that Tutu administered sometimes generated controversy. The money often originated from whites but was used to assist blacks who suffered from apartheid in some way. Tutu spent other discretionary funds on educational scholarships, families of strikers, the Release Mandela Campaign, blankets for the poor, and food for prisoners. The SACC also gave legal and financial support to detainees and trade unions.

Shortly after Tutu became head of the SACC, allegations of financial irregularities began to surface at the organization. Tutu hired outside consultants to diagnose the problem. They revealed some mismanagement among mid- and low-level staff. When Tutu tried to settle matters internally without taking the wrongdoers to court, some critics accused him of trying to launch a cover-up. He was devastated when his integrity was questioned in court and in the press, but he was never formally charged with any wrongdoing himself.

Tutu took a personal interest in his employees' background and problems. He created a warm and supportive environment for his multiracial staff, many of whom called him "Baba" (father). One black South African employee remembered that Tutu openly displayed his emotions. He liked jokes and laughter but could be moved to tears easily. He was offended by bad language, disliked gossip, and hated ethnic slurs. He gave affection willingly and needed the affection of others.[3] He also tended to trust others, even if they did not deserve it. For example, he refused to believe rumors that a government informer had been planted among the SACC staff, but years later it turned out to be true.[4]

Regular prayer and meditation continued to play an important role in Tutu's spiritual life. He woke up early each morning to pray and often worshipped at home with his wife. He also prayed before meetings and interviews. As he had throughout his career in the priesthood, he attended retreats so that he could better communicate with God. These retreats helped prepare him for important decisions and events. For Tutu, quiet reflection alone was as necessary as food and water, even though he was naturally an extrovert with other people. "Without my daily time of meditation, I am not a full person, and not prepared to face the daily challenges as a Christian," Tutu said.[5] He wanted his staff to integrate prayer into their daily lives as well. At SACC prayer sessions, Tutu insisted on praying not only for the victims of apartheid, but also for the perpetrators, even if his colleagues viewed these individuals as enemies. He continued to pray for P. W. Botha, despite staff objections, and also prayed for police officers and prison guards "because they are God's children too."[6]

The SACC's main office was located at Khotso House (house of peace) in central Johannesburg. Two visiting academics furnished this portrait of Tutu as they interviewed him there in 1980:

> As he leaned forward in his chair, we sense the energy in his solidly built, lithe body. He is short, yet gives the impression of being a big man. He has a high forehead, long nose, short cropped hair peppered with gray and lively black eyes framed by gold spectacles. He speaks with his hands—indeed, his body seems always in movement. That day he was wearing the traditional white clerical collar, silver pectoral cross, and purple shirt, with carefully pressed tweed trousers. Somehow there was a certain debonair quality in his attire and in his manner.[7]

Tutu's typical day was hectic by any measure. He arose at 4:45 A.M. and went jogging in his Soweto neighborhood at 5:30 A.M. He left home by 6:30 and arrived at St. Mary's Cathedral for Eucharist at about 7:00. After entering his office at 8:00, he read newspapers and did some devotional readings before attending staff prayers at 8:30 A.M. The rest of his day was usually filled with meetings, interviews, conferences, and occasionally formal luncheons. Tutu's staff left at 4:40 P.M., but he remained behind for reading and prayers. He was usually home by 6:00 if no additional meetings were scheduled and went to bed between 10:00 and 11:00 P.M.[8] Leah wished her husband had more time for family activities, but she fully supported his public life. She always encouraged Desmond to be somewhat irreverent so he could retain his sanity under pressure and enjoy life. Having Leah by his side helped ease the tensions and responsibilities inherent in Tutu's very high-profile position.

The Tutus' home was larger than most houses in Soweto—most of which were tiny and mass produced—but it was unremarkable by the standards of most white South African suburbs. Nor was it lavishly furnished. Tutu dressed well and drove a nice car, but as a visiting *New York Times* correspondent observed, "He is not by any stretch of the imagination a man in love with luxury."[9] Though he wasn't "in love with luxury," Tutu did have his passions. His favorite snacks were samosas (deep-fried, stuffed Indian pastries), marshmallows, fat cakes (a kind of South African pastry), dried fruit, nuts, Yogi Sip (a liquefied yogurt drink), and lime or orange juice.[10] He also enjoyed music, morning runs, afternoon naps, and the sport of cricket.

As busy as he was at the SACC, Tutu wanted to minister to his own personal flock. His wish came true after three years at the council, when he added to his responsibilities by becoming rector of St. Augustine's Church in Orlando West, Soweto. The humble church began to thrive under Tutu's stewardship. Mentoring, supporting, and encouraging his new congregation made the now well-known bishop a popular figure in his local community.

However, it didn't take long for Tutu to realize that church and state were on a collision course in South Africa. He predicted that the two institutions would inevitably clash as long as the South African government's laws were contrary to the gospel. He believed that it was his Christian duty to oppose unjust laws, as it was for Christians everywhere. Although the South African government loudly condemned those who mixed religion and politics, Tutu saw a double standard because the government did not mind when clerics from the Dutch Reformed Church endorsed apartheid. Tutu insisted that resisting apartheid was a Christian obligation. "There can be no argument whose laws must be obeyed when there is a clash between God's laws and those of man," he said.[11]

Tutu did not view the SACC as a political organization, although it would often be charged as such. He said that all of the council's activities sprung from Christian principles, especially the commandment to love "our neighbor as ourselves." As he put it, "We in the SACC believe in a nonracial South Africa where people count because they are made in the image of God. So the SACC is neither a black nor a white organization. It is a Christian organization with a definite bias in favor of the oppressed and the exploited ones of our society."[12] Tutu viewed himself as a spokesman for black South Africans but denied having political ambitions. He consistently said that Nelson Mandela (imprisoned since 1962) was the most widely respected political leader in the black community.

Under Tutu's leadership, the SACC not only condemned apartheid in general terms, it protested specific government policies. It criticized pass-law arrests, forced removals, the lack of educational facilities for black students in Soweto, and violence in South-West Africa (the South African military was trying to destroy a liberation movement there that opposed South African control of the territory). Tutu also pledged the SACC's support to a number of welfare organizations. He encouraged the Black Sash (an antiapartheid organization led by white women) to set up advice centers for black South Africans throughout the country. He also established a council to help black South Africans become educated overseas and develop skills needed back home. One of Tutu's highest priorities was his campaign against forced removals. Three million black South Africans had been forced from their homes between 1960 and 1980 and taken to homelands, which they had often never seen before and to which they had no connection. Tutu visited uprooted communities, met with residents, and spoke out publicly on their behalf. He was appalled that people could be deprived of their right to land, liberty, and property by a government that claimed to be Christian. He ensured that the SACC supported victims of forced removals both financially and spiritually.

In 1979, the SACC encouraged its members to consider civil disobedience to express their opposition to apartheid. Tutu endorsed the proposal. The government then warned the council not to encourage people to break the law and scolded Tutu during a private meeting. Instead of backing down, Tutu dared the government to prosecute Christians. The government refused to accept the dare—at least for the time being.

Tutu's public profile rose steadily in the late 1970s, largely because of his frequent speeches and interviews. One prominent South African magazine editor even remarked, "That man makes more speeches than he eats breakfasts."[13] Tutu's voice and manner could light up an audience; he never sounded puritanical or humorless. In 1980, he shocked some observers by predicting that South Africa would have a black prime minister within 5 or 10 years. During a speech at Stellenbosch University, Tutu told Afrikaner students that blacks did not want "crumbs of concessions from a generous master, they wanted to be at the table, planning the menu with him."[14] Tutu believed the whole edifice of apartheid had to be dismantled—pass laws, homelands, forced removals, Bantu education, and unequal citizenship. The easing of segregation in some public places was not enough. He spoke out against banning and detention without trial and often warned the government what might happen if it continued to treat blacks so contemptuously. Blacks could eventually become so dehumanized and bitter, he said, that they might become unforgiving and violent themselves. Tutu was careful not to threaten or endorse violence, however. He just predicted that South Africa could explode if changes were not made quickly enough.

Tutu described himself as a man of peace, not a pacifist. He suggested that violence had been necessary to stop the Nazis during World War II, but he sought to do all he could to stop violence from escalating in South Africa. He condemned acts of violence perpetrated by both the government and the antiapartheid movement. Too many white South Africans criticized violence from the latter group, Tutu argued, without criticizing the structural violence waged against blacks in the form of police brutality, pass laws, and the deaths of innocent women and children.

One nonviolent strategy that Tutu began to advocate was foreign economic pressure. His decision to back this approach was prompted by a conversation he had with a young black girl at a forced relocation camp in the eastern Cape in June 1979. Here is how Tutu described the encounter: "I met this little girl who lives with her widowed mother and sister. I asked whether her mother received a pension or any other grant and she said, 'No.' 'Then how do you live?' I asked. 'We borrow food,' she said. 'Have you ever returned the food you borrowed?' 'No.' 'What happens if you can't borrow food?' 'We drink water to fill our stomachs.'" Tutu believed that the calculated imposition of this kind of suffering was truly "diabolical."[15]

During an interview on Danish television a few months later, Tutu said it was "rather disgraceful" that Denmark bought South African coal.[16] This remark generated enormous controversy in South Africa. Soweto civic leaders supported Tutu, but the white community and the government were outraged. In October 1979, Tutu was summoned to Pretoria to see the minister of justice and other officials, who told him that his remarks amounted to economic sabotage. They ordered him to retract his statement and apologize. After the meeting, Tutu conferred with other church leaders who offered him their support. He decided not to waver. He would neither retract his statement nor apologize. Once his decision was announced, Tutu's profile among black South Africans rose significantly. He then reiterated his belief that foreign economic pressure could weaken apartheid. Regarding his remarks on Danish television, Tutu said, "It has been a horrible pain to experience the hatred, vituperation and hostility of whites because of my Denmark coal statement. If I could have released only a fraction of the feeling against resettlements and population removals that my Danish statement did, I would sing Alleluia."[17]

Tutu wanted multinational corporations to do more to improve conditions in South Africa. Their presence would be acceptable if they gave their workforce better housing, invested in black education and training, and expressed opposition to the homelands policy. Tutu did not yet call for foreign companies to withdraw completely from South Africa.

Tutu's outspoken criticisms of apartheid angered the government, the press, and large sections of the white South African public. In 1979–80, the right-wing Christian League received R340,000 ($442,000) from the government to wage a propaganda offensive against the SACC. The government was so suspicious of Tutu and other antiapartheid Christians that it even ordered its security police to establish an office "specializing in theological matters."[18] The government put the SACC under surveillance, ordered the police to raid SACC offices, and used radio and television to demonize the organization and its leaders. The state-run South African Broadcasting Company (SABC) regularly demeaned Tutu and distorted his views. Once SABC-TV showed Tutu rubbing his hands while he was giving testimony before a government commission in order to imply that he was nervous or untrustworthy. The habit actually arose from his bout with tuberculosis as a teenager, which weakened the hand that he rubbed periodically. White-owned newspapers often pilloried Tutu. One newspaper referred to him as "that insect in dark glasses." Another ran a photo of Tutu with the headline, "Fingers in the Till," as if to suggest that he had been involved in unethical financial conduct.[19] Letters to the editor frequently accused him of promoting communism.

With such hostility emanating from the government and the press, it's no wonder that many whites viewed Tutu with hostility. In an appearance before the Pretoria press club, Tutu recognized that whites tended to view him as "an irresponsible, radical fire-eater who should have been locked up long ago."[20] He received plenty of hate mail. He would reply if the letters were phrased reasonably and tended to ignore the less-temperate letters. Sometimes he would reply angrily if the letters were unduly nasty. Most of the critics were conservative white South Africans who opposed his calls for change. They could not accept that a black South African occupied such a prominent leadership position in the church. Many whites despised Tutu because they believed he advocated revolution, when he actually warned against impending revolution and violence. For someone who valued being admired, Tutu was deeply troubled by people's hatred. But he wasn't afraid to criticize white audiences. In one speech he urged his white listeners not to behave like bullies. They should realize their self-worth without devaluing the worth of others, he said.

The harassment Tutu experienced could make his life difficult. He received many death threats and obscene telephone calls. Once when he was in the Johannesburg airport, a white woman who spotted him said that if she had a gun she would shoot him.[21] Sometimes people who attended his speeches were harassed. At other times the government encouraged people to circulate libelous pamphlets about him and the SACC. Tutu's family was also victimized. Occasionally, hostile callers who intended to speak to Tutu made their threats when his children answered the phone. Police searched Desmond, Leah, and their daughters a few times, but their favorite target was Trevor, the Tutus' eldest child. He was regularly stopped by police and arrested for no other reason than being Desmond Tutu's son. "In order to get at me, they would go for my family; that was very painful," Tutu later recalled. He knew early on that he might have to suffer because of his high-profile activism, but he didn't originally realize that his family would have to suffer as well. His wife and children tended to accept that this was part of their contribution to the struggle. Tutu, on the other hand, would feel anguish about it for years to come.[22]

At least Tutu could be heartened by the support he received from the black community. When he returned from Britain in 1975, he wasn't well known enough to have been considered a leader by most black South Africans. But when the government started condemning him during his tenure at the SACC, his reputation among black South Africans soared. Clearly, the government's criticism backfired. Far from discrediting Tutu, their attacks only brought him more black admiration. He received a flood of letters from black South Africans requesting his assistance, participation, and advice. His fearless public stance against apartheid made him an icon in South Africa, at least in the eyes of apartheid's many victims. Some black South Africans thought Tutu was too moderate, however. They believed he spent too much time trying to cultivate white goodwill. "The trouble with Desmond," one ANC activist said, "is that he really thinks the whites can be converted." A young black Catholic priest who supported the black consciousness movement said this about Tutu: "He will say 'Love your enemy.' At his age, he should hate a little more. There's this problem with Tutu—he believes in the Gospel literally." Even Tutu's daughter Naomi admitted that sometimes she became frustrated by her father's "attempts to teach us that hating someone else is like hating ourselves and God."[23] Tutu faced the perpetual dilemma of all moderates—he was often viewed suspiciously by the two hostile sides he sought to bring together.

Tutu refused to be silent, despite the pressures and criticisms he faced. He believed he was doing God's work in speaking out against injustice and promoting racial reconciliation. The prayers he received from the worldwide Christian community gave him the strength he needed to carry on. Sometimes even his family was amazed by his fortitude. "Leah, with typical wry humor, is sure that even if his tongue were cut off, he would not be prevented from speaking," one writer noted. Tutu did not let his family's concern go unanswered. "My wife and mother say, 'Why do you talk so much?' But I say if it's my destiny to speak out, I'd rather be happy in prison than unfree when I'm free."[24]

Soon Tutu had the opportunity to prove his point. In May 1980, a mixed-race Congregationalist minister, John Thorne, was arrested in the Johannesburg area for speaking at a meeting concerning a black school boycott. The SACC organized a demonstration to protest the minister's arrest. As Tutu and 34 other clerics marched toward police headquarters at John Vorster Square in Johannesburg, they were confronted by armed police and charged with violating the Riotous Assemblies Act. The police then arrested the churchmen and held them in jail overnight. Tutu used the occasion to pray, sing hymns, and talk with his fellow clerics throughout the night. The next day they were fined and released—and so was Rev. Thorne.

During his brushes with authority, Tutu was buoyed by letters of support from around the world. These letters convinced him that he and his colleagues were part of one large, extended Christian family. Such support kept Tutu's spirits from sinking when the government refused to issue him a passport from March 1980 to January 1981. As Tutu described it, "I was overwhelmed by messages of sympathy and support from all over the world, but nothing touched me more than to get from the Sunday school children at St. James's, Madison Avenue, in New York what the children called passports of love, which I pasted up on the wall of my office. How can anyone range himself against this international, this global fellowship?"[25]

Even though Tutu predicted a bleak future for South Africa if it didn't change course, he still believed that goodness would ultimately prevail. He marveled at how blacks were still generally forgiving, even after generations of discrimination. He believed that most blacks wanted to live in harmony with their white fellow citizens. Ironically, Tutu's critics charged him with deliberately inciting racial conflict, when he wanted to promote racial reconciliation. He tried to cultivate goodwill from whites in general and those in the Dutch Reformed Church (DRC) in particular. So many Afrikaners in the apartheid government had been members of the DRC that the church was sometimes called "the National Party at prayer." Tutu understood that their journey away from racial prejudice would be a difficult one. He regularly expressed his gratitude toward white officials when he believed their actions warranted it. He praised or thanked P. W. Botha and his cabinet ministers for concessions on various occasions and reacted positively when political prisoners were given more study privileges. He even told audiences that the police had a responsibility to maintain law and order.

Tutu's belief in the need for a constructive, peaceful dialogue with whites was the essence of his moderation. During his tenure at the SACC, more radical blacks felt the time for talking was over—they wanted revolution instead. But not Tutu. He spoke to as many white audiences as he could, urging them to support the struggle against apartheid so they could join the "winning side." He spoke at both Afrikaans and English-speaking universities. In a 1980 speech at the University of the Witwatersrand in Johannesburg, Tutu urged white students to help "uproot all evil and oppression and injustice of which blacks are victims and whites are beneficiaries."[26] Sometimes he convinced his listeners, but not always. At one church conference, Tutu wept openly because whites seemed so hardhearted and reluctant to accept black goodwill.[27]

Tutu's third year as SACC general secretary was a turbulent one for South Africa. In 1980, student boycotts in schools and universities severely disrupted the country's educational system. Tutu proposed that a high-level SACC delegation seek a meeting with Prime Minister Botha to discuss the deteriorating situation. Such a proposal risked alienating black South Africans who distrusted the government; it also risked the SACC's credibility. Botha agreed to meet the SACC delegation only if the council explicitly rejected communism, violence, and the ANC. In response, the SACC issued a statement saying that it had never endorsed communism or violence and that it was not in an alliance with the ANC. The meeting with the prime minister was held on August 7, 1980. Tutu's delegation included SACC senior leaders and representatives of member churches; Botha's team included several members of the cabinet. Tutu urged the government to take a number of steps to defuse the growing bitterness in the country. It should grant common citizenship to all South Africans, end population removals, lift the pass laws, and establish a single education system. According to Tutu, if Botha took these steps, he would "go down in history as a truly great man."[28] The meeting was civil, but Botha did not take Tutu's proposals seriously. He vaguely agreed to explore "new dispensations" but rejected "one person one vote" in a unitary state. Before the meeting ended, he warned church leaders to avoid engaging in hostile antigovernment rhetoric.

Some radical black theologians said afterward that future meetings with the government would be pointless. They viewed Tutu as naive for having tried to negotiate with a government so hostile to black interests. Other blacks strongly criticized Tutu for meeting with "the enemy." But

Tutu was undaunted. Even though this first meeting with the Botha government had not produced concrete results, he would not rule out trying again. His career as a bridge builder would continue, despite South Africa's steadily escalating racial conflict.

Tutu didn't restrict his activism just to high-level meetings and conferences. Sometimes he intervened in situations that were much riskier. In Soweto, he once rushed to protect an elderly man who was being assaulted by two white policemen. The policemen stopped in disbelief as Tutu forced himself between them and the victim with his cross in his hand. Another dangerous situation arose during the funeral of prominent civil rights lawyer Griffiths Mxenge. The funeral service, held outdoors near King William's Town on December 2, 1981, drew 15,000 angry mourners, many of whom correctly suspected that Mxenge had been murdered by a government death squad. Some mourners spotted a black security policeman in their midst. Like a swarm of angry bees, the crowd closed in on the alleged traitor and began attacking him. Tutu, who was one of the speakers at the funeral, rushed over to protect the victim by shielding him with his body. When the crowd's anger seemed to dissipate, Tutu returned to the speakers' platform. But later, the policeman was dragged off and killed, despite Tutu's attempts to save him. This incident triggered Tutu's fears that blacks were losing patience with his words of peace and nonviolence. Blacks were becoming so angry—particularly at those who collaborated with "the system"—that violence seemed inevitable, despite Tutu's effort to stop it. Before he left Mxenge's funeral, Tutu told mourners that the struggle was far from over: "Many more will be detained. Many more will be banned. Many more will be deported and killed. Yes, it will be costly. But we shall be free. Nothing will stop us from becoming free—no police bullets, dogs, tear-gas, prison, death, no nothing will stop us because God is on our side."[29]

Finally the government had had enough of this outspoken black clergyman. It decided to publicly demonize Tutu and silence him once and for all. In November 1981, Prime Minister Botha established an official commission of inquiry to investigate the SACC under the chairmanship of C. F. Eloff, a Transvaal judge. The all-white commission was asked to investigate the council's activities, finances, and personnel in an implicit effort to undermine the SACC and its controversial leader. It sought to uncover financial mismanagement and treasonable activities, to link the SACC to foreign-inspired conspiracies against South Africa, to discredit and embarrass the SACC, and to erode its support both domestically and internationally. The head of the security police, Johan Coetzee, believed that the council should be declared an "affected organization" and made subject to the Fund Raising Act. This would cut off the SACC's overseas funding and allow the government to control the organization's finances. Despite its grave misgivings, the SACC decided to cooperate fully with the inquiry.

Tutu was determined not to let the government intimidate him. He would continue to speak out while the Eloff Commission was conducting its investigation. For example, on June 16, 1982, just months after the commission began its work, Tutu attended a special service at Regina Mundi Church in Soweto to commemorate the sixth anniversary of the 1976 unrest. Police cordoned off the church in an effort to intimidate those who wanted to attend. They also arrested journalists who tried to cover the service. Ever defiant, Tutu asked the 5,000 people in the audience, "Is there anyone here who doubts that apartheid is doomed to failure?" "No!" shouted the audience in reply. "Is there anyone who doubts we are going to be free?" "No!" the people yelled. Then Tutu urged the crowd to chant, "We are going to be free! We are going to be free!"[30] Tutu later tried to restrain the people's anger by stopping them from throwing stones at the police. Eventually the police stormed into the churchyard chasing and beating people, injuring Tutu's daughter Naomi and her fiancé in the process. "When we got home," Naomi wrote,

> I asked my father, "Can you still ask us to forgive? Can you still believe they are our brothers, that we have some responsibility to them?" He had no profound statement that will be remembered for generations, but simply said, "I cannot ask you to do anything since you were the one beaten, but I hope that if I am ever the one, I will still be able to forgive and pray for them. That is the strength I ask for."[31]

Tutu gave evidence at the Eloff Commission's first public hearing in Pretoria in September 1982. His statement revealed his whole approach to theology. Because the "central work of Jesus" was to bring about reconciliation "between man and man," apartheid was unchristian because it treated some as less human than others. Tutu viewed it as his duty—and that of all Christians—to obey the laws of God, even if they conflicted with the laws of man. He believed that the SACC wasn't just being investigated, but that Christianity itself was on trial. "The Bible is the most revolutionary, the most radical book there is," Tutu told the commission. "If a book had to be banned, then it ought to have been the Bible, by those who rule unjustly and as tyrants. Whites brought us the Bible and we are taking it seriously."[32]

The Eloff Commission had no authority over Christian churches, Tutu insisted, because only churches knew how to interpret the gospel. Since the SACC had broken no laws, it would continue its work, and so would Tutu himself. His loyalty to God over man was unequivocal:

> I want the government to know now and always that I do not fear them. They are trying to defend the utterly indefensible. Apartheid is as evil and as vicious as Nazism and Communism and the government will fail completely for it is ranging itself on the side of evil, injustice, and oppression. The government is not God, just ordinary human beings who very soon, like other tyrants before them, will bite the dust.

Tutu almost seemed to be inviting the government's wrath, but he vowed to continue to speak out as long as he was able. He declared,

> There is nothing the government can do to me that will stop me from being involved in what I believe is what God wants me to do. I will not keep quiet, for as Jeremiah says, when I try to keep quiet God's word burns like a fire in my breast. But what is it that they can ultimately do? The most awful thing that they can do is to kill me, and death is not the worst thing that can happen to a Christian.

The main point of Tutu's testimony was simple: the SACC's outspokenness on social issues derived from spiritual obligations, not political goals. To be good Christians, the council's leadership must encourage people to love their neighbors. "I want to assure you that we are not politicians," Tutu told the commission. "We are attempting to be decent Christians."[33]

Tutu's lack of personal bitterness revealed itself one day during a tea break. He walked up to Johan Coetzee to congratulate him on being promoted to commissioner of police (he was formerly head of the security police). Coetzee was at the hearings to testify against Tutu and the SACC, whom he charged were supporting the climate of violence in South Africa. Tutu's magnanimous gesture showed that he did not view whites as enemies, even if they enforced apartheid.

The magnanimity was not mutual. One of the government's strategies was to embarrass the SACC over financial irregularities in the organization. Some donations were unaccounted for in the council's records. Tutu's finances also came under scrutiny, especially the $15,000 he had been given to renovate his Soweto house. Tutu was originally told that the money came from a West German donor who wished to remain anonymous. The government tried to use Tutu's middle-class lifestyle to suggest that he was a rich priest living the good life while his people suffered. When it was revealed that the donation had not come from overseas but from a former SACC official's fraudulent account, Tutu returned the money immediately.

Both the SACC and Tutu himself received strong international backing during the inquiry. European donors flew thousands of miles to testify on behalf of the council. The archbishop of Canterbury, Robert Runcie, sent an Anglican delegation to the hearings composed of English, Scottish, American, Canadian, and New Zealand representatives who were eager to support the SACC. "If you touch Desmond Tutu," Archbishop Runcie declared, "you touch a world family of Christians."[34] Tutu was supremely grateful that the government's attempts to smear the SACC were rejected by both the Church of England and many others in the wider world.

The Eloff Commission published its report in February 1984. It said that the SACC was more concerned with political, social, and economic matters than spiritual matters and that it had adopted a number of positions contrary to the national interest on matters such as disinvestment, conscientious objection, and civil disobedience. It also accused the SACC of trying to conceal its reliance on overseas funding. However, the commission did not recommend that the council be considered an "affected organization" because this would have been seen as an attack on religious freedom. In addition, commissioners feared that the government would lose face if it cut off the SACC's funding. The South African government clearly hadn't expected that the SACC would enjoy such a groundswell of support from black South Africans or overseas sympathizers. Some high-ranking government officials were disappointed in the toothlessness of the Eloff Commission's final report. After its publication, Minister of Law and Order Louis Le Grange said, "I warn him [Tutu] and the SACC that...I will not allow any wicked acts to be committed under the cloak of religion."[35]

Tutu was defiant to the end. He responded that no government had the right to tell churches how to interpret the gospel. If the SACC had broken any laws, he said, it should have been charged in court. But now was not the time for recriminations. Although the SACC's work had been interrupted and its affairs scrutinized, Tutu and his colleagues felt a sense of vindication and triumph after the publication of the commission's report. They were enormously pleased that they had received such widespread support from their friends and that they could continue their work unhindered.

Under Tutu's leadership, the South African Council of Churches had become a major player in the struggle to end apartheid. The organization had steadily gained new support at home and abroad since Tutu became general secretary in 1978. Black South Africans began to view the SACC as a major ally in their quest for democracy and human rights, largely because of Tutu's leadership, courage, and determination. His rising profile in South Africa was underscored in 1981 when he was nominated to become the first black archbishop of Cape Town. The Anglican Church assembly became deadlocked over who to appoint, fearing that Tutu's selection would trigger white flight and confrontation with the government. Although the assembly eventually settled on another (white) candidate, that they even considered Tutu was a milestone. By the 1980s, Tutu's stature among black South Africans was rivaled by only one man—Nelson Mandela.

NOTES

1. Brian Pottinger, *The Imperial Presidency: P.W. Botha—The First 10 Years* (Johannesburg: Southern Book Publishers, 1988), p. 133.

2. Joseph Lelyveld, "South Africa's Bishop Tutu," *New York Times Magazine*, 14 March 1982, p. 42.

3. Sophie Mazibuko, "Archbishop Tutu—The Man," in *Hammering Swords Into Ploughshares: Essays in Honor of Archbishop Mpilo Desmond Tutu*, ed. Buti Tlhagale and Itumeleng Mosala (Grand Rapids, MI: William B. Eerdmans, 1987), pp. 13–18.

4. Shirley du Boulay, *Tutu: Voice of the Voiceless* (Grand Rapids, MI: William B. Eerdmans, 1988), p. 134.

5. J. H. P. Serfontein, "Tutu—The Man of Peace," *Ecunews* 8 (December 1984): p. 19.

6. Quoted in du Boulay, *Tutu*, p. 140.

7. Marjorie Hope and James Young, "Desmond Mpilo Tutu: South Africa's Doughty Black Bishop," *Christian Century* 97, no. 43 (31 December 1980): p. 1291.

8. Hope and Young, "Desmond Mpilo Tutu," p. 1292.

9. Lelyveld, "South Africa's Bishop Tutu," p. 44.

10. Mazibuko, "Archbishop Tutu—The Man," p. 18.

11. Desmond Tutu, *The Rainbow People of God: The Making of a Peaceful Revolution*, ed. John Allen (New York: Doubleday, 1994), p. 33.

12. Tutu, *The Rainbow People of God*, p. 36.

13. Quoted in Lelyveld, "South Africa's Bishop Tutu," p. 25. The editor was Denis Beckett.

14. Quoted in du Boulay, *Tutu*, p. 165.

15. Tutu, *The Rainbow People of God*, pp. 25–26.

16. Tutu, *The Rainbow People of God*, p. 26.

17. Tutu, *The Rainbow People of God*, p. 39.

18. Lelyveld, "South Africa's Bishop Tutu," p. 42.

19. Du Boulay, *Tutu*, pp. 139 and 182.

20. Quoted in du Boulay, *Tutu*, p. 166.

21. Quoted in du Boulay, *Tutu*, p. 139.

22. Desmond Tutu, in discussion with the author, 29 April 2003, Jacksonville, FL.

23. Richard John Neuhaus, *Dispensations: The Future of South Africa as South Africans See It* (Grand Rapids, MI: William B. Eerdmans, 1986), p. 133; Lelyveld, "South Africa's Bishop Tutu," p. 102; and Naomi Tutu, "Introduction" in *The Words of Desmond Tutu* (New York: Newmarket Press, 1989), p. 17.

24. Du Boulay, *Tutu*, p. 157 and Judith Bentley, *Archbishop Tutu of South Africa* (Hillside, NJ: Enslow, 1988), p. 66.

25. Tutu, *The Rainbow People of God*, p. 74.

26. Du Boulay, *Tutu*, p. 161.

27. Lelyveld, "South Africa's Bishop Tutu," p. 25.

28. Tutu, *The Rainbow People of God*, p. 44.

29. Du Boulay, *Tutu*, p. 163.

30. Du Boulay, *Tutu*, pp. 168–69.

31. Naomi Tutu, *The Words of Desmond Tutu*, pp. 17–18.

32. Serfontein, "Tutu—The Man of Peace," p. 19.

33. Tutu, *The Rainbow People of God*, pp. 54–79.

34. Du Boulay, *Tutu*, p. 176.

35. Du Boulay, *Tutu*, p. 178.

Chapter 10

RISING INTERNATIONAL PROFILE

As the leader of the South African Council of Churches, Tutu became well known not just in South Africa, but all over the world. He began to receive invitations to meet with government officials and address universities and churches in an ever-growing number of foreign countries from the late 1970s onward. In accepting as many of these invitations as he could, Tutu educated the world about the problems facing South Africa. His central message remained constant—that apartheid was immoral because it violated God's teachings that all belonged to one human family.

In a speech to the Royal Commonwealth Society in Britain in 1978, Tutu left no doubt that black South Africans would eventually gain their freedom. Once they did, he maintained, they would remember who their friends were. He believed that the door to peaceful change was closing and that if change didn't come soon, white fears of violence and mayhem would become a self-fulfilling prophecy. But he insisted that blacks had no desire to drive whites into the sea. Tutu had a knack for keeping his listeners spellbound. One American priest observed that when Tutu spoke, "everyone feels the electricity as if a 220 volt wire had suddenly been plugged in."[1]

Soon Tutu began to collect awards and honorary degrees, particularly in Britain and the United States. In 1978 he was elected as a fellow of King's College, London, the institution where he had studied in the 1960s. That same year, two institutions awarded him honorary doctorates: General Theological Seminary in New York and the University of Kent in Britain. When he received an honorary doctorate of law from Harvard University in 1979, the 20,000 members of the audience gave him a

standing ovation. The honors Tutu received—and would continue to receive—indicated the growing esteem with which he was regarded by the
outside world.

In May 1979, Desmond and Leah traveled to Newark, New Jersey, so
that Tutu could work with the Episcopalian bishop John Spong. Bishop
Spong had first met Tutu during a trip to South Africa in 1976, shortly
after the Soweto unrest began. He participated in Tutu's consecration as
bishop of Lesotho at St. Mary's Cathedral in Johannesburg. Spong would
serve as bishop of Newark for more than 20 years and became a well-
known advocate of progressive, inclusive Christianity. He and Tutu developed a strong friendship that deepened over the years. In fact, Tutu
would return to Spong's diocese several years later to serve as assistant
bishop. During his 1979 stay in the United States, Tutu spoke out against
apartheid in numerous speeches on the East Coast but refrained from calling directly for economic sanctions. It was later that year, during his visit
to Denmark, that Tutu made headlines by criticizing the Danes for buying
South African coal. By the early 1980s, Tutu regularly suggested that foreign economic pressure was needed to force the South African government to abandon apartheid. Until the government felt uncomfortable, he
reasoned, apartheid would continue. Opponents of foreign pressure argued that such measures would cost some black South Africans their jobs.
Tutu would reply that blacks were already suffering, and they would be
willing to suffer a little more if it meant that real change lay ahead.

Tutu's popularity in Europe and North America might have made South
African officials reluctant to ban or detain him, but the government frequently restricted his ability to travel. It first seized Tutu's passport in
March 1980 in retaliation for his comments in Denmark. But the attempt
to neutralize him backfired. Once word of the seizure spread to the outside
world, messages of support for Tutu flooded in from the United Nations,
the United States, the United Kingdom, and elsewhere. In a speech to the
South African Parliament, member of Parliament Helen Suzman said that
the action would infuriate blacks, many other South Africans, and supporters of freedom worldwide. Tutu's passport was returned in early 1981,
10 months after it had been withdrawn. His passport said that his nationality was "undeterminable at present" because he had grown up in a multi-
ethnic household. The South African government preferred to categorize
blacks into distinct ethnic groups rather than classify them as South
African citizens. Tutu always insisted that he was a South African and not
affiliated to any homeland or particular tribal group.

Once he received his passport back in 1981, Tutu conducted an extensive tour of Europe and the United States to convince the world to put

pressure on the South African government. He traveled to Switzerland, West Germany, Sweden, Norway, and Denmark before arriving in the United States. There, he met UN Secretary General Kurt Waldheim and addressed the UN's special committee against apartheid. He also met with the U.S. ambassador to the UN, Jeanne Kirkpatrick. Tutu then flew to Britain for meetings and interviews. During a sermon at Westminster Abbey in London, he criticized western countries for supporting the status quo in South Africa. He wondered aloud whether these countries were engaged in "a conspiracy to keep South African blacks in bondage."[2] Before returning home, Tutu met Pope John Paul II in Rome. When he arrived back in South Africa in April 1981, a crowd gathered at the Johannesburg airport to welcome him home. The government was less than pleased. It promptly withdrew his passport again and refused to reissue it for another 17 months.

Despite the repeated confiscations of his passport, Tutu refused to muzzle his criticisms of apartheid. But the restrictions did prevent him from accepting many invitations to overseas conferences and award ceremonies in the early 1980s. He was unable to travel to Aberdeen University in Scotland and Ruhr University in West Germany to receive honorary degrees in person, nor could he receive the honorary doctorate of law at Columbia University. Columbia did not award honorary degrees in absentia, so when Tutu could not attend the commencement ceremony in May 1982, the university left an empty chair on the stage to affirm its solidarity with Tutu. University officials then decided that if Tutu wasn't allowed to come to them, they would go to him. In August 1982, Columbia's president and two trustees traveled to Johannesburg, where they awarded Tutu his honorary degree at a special ceremony at the University of the Witwatersrand.

In September 1982, Tutu was invited to address the Triennial Convention of the Episcopal Church in New Orleans. The South African government initially denied him permission to travel, but when U.S. Vice President George Bush urged them to reconsider, officials in Pretoria reversed themselves and let Tutu go. Tutu did not call for economic sanctions to be applied against South Africa during that trip, but he had not become acquiescent. He told the delegates that, far from abandoning apartheid, the government had merely reformed it. He held no grudges, however. "The people who are perpetrators of injury in our land are not sporting horns or tails," he said. "They're just ordinary people who are scared. Wouldn't you be scared if you were outnumbered five to one?" Delegates gave Tutu a 15-minute standing ovation. "I think even if I had said 'Rub a dub dub' they would have given me a standing ovation," Tutu quipped later.[3] He had clearly become a hero, not just to many American Episcopalians, but to many Americans period. After the conference in New Orleans, Desmond and Leah visited Kentucky, where their daughter Naomi lived with her American husband. In an interview, Tutu said that the situation in South Africa had deteriorated in the five years since the death of Steve Biko. He suggested that the United States could do more to pressure the South African government to grant blacks equal rights.

South Africa had never been in the forefront of U.S. foreign policy. The first sustained American movement to pressure the South African government arose in the late 1970s after the Soweto unrest. Students, African American leaders, and other activists began to pressure universities and city councils to withdraw their investments in American companies that did business in South Africa to exert economic pressure on the apartheid government. The Carter administration and UN ambassador Andrew Young criticized apartheid more vocally than had previous administrations, but their words did little to change Pretoria's mindset.

The Reagan administration came into office with a new South African policy known as "constructive engagement." It was devised by Chester Crocker, the new assistant secretary of state for African affairs. Under constructive engagement, the United States toned down its harsh criticisms of South Africa and pursued quiet diplomacy instead. Reagan officials believed that because the South African government was a key Cold War ally in the global struggle against communism, it should not be unduly antagonized. Crocker also had faith in P. W. Botha's cautious reforms and believed that U.S. economic pressure would make the government more intransigent. Because the white minority government was so strong, Crocker reasoned, it could not be bullied by external or internal forces. He said that while the United States did not support apartheid, cutting ties to the South African government would be like walking away from the problem. Under the Reagan administration, the American delegation at the UN would oppose harsh measures to punish or isolate South Africa. The White House also resisted calls to impose sanctions on South Africa. In 1982, the Reagan administration approved the sale of aircraft to the South African police and military. It also approved the sale of computers to the military and homeland administrations. That year, Herman Nickel was appointed U.S. ambassador to South Africa. He was a strong advocate of U.S. investment in South Africa and believed that American companies promoted positive change and economic growth. The policy of constructive engagement gradually became more controversial, especially when unrest in South Africa escalated.

Tutu was troubled by the new policy from the start. During his 1982 trip to the United States, Tutu met with Chester Crocker to discuss U.S. policy toward South Africa. In a public statement, Tutu acknowledged the Reagan administration's role in enabling him to appear at the Episcopal convention in New Orleans but said that despite constructive engagement, repression in South Africa had continued unchecked. He described the South African government's proposed "orderly movement and settlement of black persons" bill as "the National Party's final solution for blacks, rather as the Nazis had a final solution for Jews."[4] Assistant Secretary Crocker realized that Tutu was a force to be reckoned with. He later referred to Tutu as "the courageous South African prelate with the sharp tongue."[5]

After his 1982 trip to the United States, Tutu was invited to preach at St. Paul's Cathedral in London, but once again the government denied him permission to travel, despite a vigorous campaign on his behalf in Britain. He was allowed to attend the Sixth Assembly of the World Council of Churches in Vancouver in mid-1983, however. The crowd listened in awe as Tutu spoke of the struggle in South Africa. An American Episcopal bishop commented that Tutu "is par excellence a dramatist when he's speaking, and when he gets serious he takes you to the top of the mountain and you weep with him. He plays every emotional chord there is in the human body."[6]

Tutu had begun to develop a real following among many North Americans concerned with racial justice. He established close ties with several Episcopal congregations in New York City in particular. Members of these churches deeply admired Tutu's commitment to justice, his spirituality, and his personal compassion. Tutu helped educate the wider American public about conditions in South Africa to a greater extent than anyone had before. Although many of his listeners immediately saw parallels between American and South African history, Tutu reminded American audiences of an important difference between the two countries. In the United States, blacks struggled to claim civil rights guaranteed them by the Constitution. In South Africa, blacks had no civil rights guaranteed by law; they were struggling for basic human rights in a system rigged against them.

Even though Tutu developed a wide following in the United States, not all Americans admired him. Rev. Jerry Falwell, the leader of the Christian lobbying group Moral Majority, publicly criticized Tutu. So did Reagan administration officials such as Patrick Buchanan. They said he was too supportive of the ANC, which they viewed as a communist organization engaged in terrorism. Tutu's decision to support economic sanctions was widely criticized by white American businessmen, but many black Americans supported Tutu's stand. Philadelphia pastor Leon Sullivan greatly admired Tutu, even though the two didn't always agree on economic policy. Sullivan believed that American businesses could exert a positive influence in South Africa if they created a nondiscriminatory workplace and actively promoted black training and advancement. Tutu reminded some black Americans of Martin Luther King Jr., the famed civil rights leader of the 1950s and '60s. Both were fearless, outspoken church leaders who fought for racial justice; both believed in nonviolence; both reached out to whites; both were gifted orators. Although flattered by the comparison, Tutu himself never dwelled on it.[7]

Tutu's frequent travels to the United States and elsewhere did not mean that he lost touch with events in South Africa. On the contrary, new political developments back home began to demand his urgent attention. In November 1983, white South African voters approved a constitutional referendum that paved the way for a new tricameral parliament. Drafted by the Botha government, the constitution established a parliament with chambers for whites, Coloureds (mixed-raced South Africans), and Indians in place of the old whites-only parliament. Sometimes the chambers would meet separately to deliberate on their own affairs, but when they met together in a joint sitting, the white members of Parliament would outnumber the mixed-race and Indian members combined. Not only was white control guaranteed, but the office of prime minister was certain to remain in white hands and would be converted into a state president with greatly expanded powers. Botha heralded the plan as evidence that South Africa was moving away from apartheid. He promised to give the African majority a greater role in governing their townships but excluded them from the new parliament. Both residential and educational segregation remained in place, as did the homelands and forced removals. In short, Botha wanted to change South Africa as long as much remained the same. This inconsistency would eventually trigger a major backlash, both in South Africa and in the wider world.

When Botha declared that South Africa's future would no longer be determined by whites alone, Tutu initially expressed admiration for the prime minister's courage. But he felt tremendously disappointed when the government's constitutional proposals excluded the African majority. Tutu would be instrumental in convincing the world that the changes Botha introduced were merely cosmetic. During a speech at the University of Cape Town in 1983, Tutu said that the proposals not only failed to diminish white control, they actually entrenched racial divisions. He called the plan "a sure recipe for national disaster." He also criticized the

American and British governments for endorsing Botha's plan. "The Reagan administration I have written off as an unmitigated disaster for us blacks," he said.[8] Tutu's frustration mirrored that of most other black South Africans. By raising expectations and then not following through, Botha unwittingly unleashed a tidal wave of black anger.

Soon a new organization arose to coordinate opposition to the tricameral parliament—the United Democratic Front (UDF). Formed in 1983, the UDF linked a broad spectrum of civic organizations together, including women's groups, Christians, workers, and students. It was a multiracial coalition whose members pledged to work together to undermine apartheid and support democracy in South Africa. The UDF backed many of the goals of the outlawed ANC but did not advocate armed struggle. Instead, its main tactics would be boycotts, strikes, and protest demonstrations. The UDF greatly energized the antiapartheid movement in South Africa and gained massive support throughout the country in the next few years. Tutu became one of the movement's patrons.

Protests in South Africa gained momentum in August 1984, when Coloured and Indian voters boycotted elections to the tricameral parliament in large numbers. The constitution was officially implemented in September 1984. That month, rent boycotts began in black townships south of Johannesburg. Some strikes began as well. In an attempt to snuff out the protests before they could spread, police fired on demonstrators, killing 60 people by the end of the month. A new period of unrest had begun in South Africa, more serious and prolonged than anything the country had ever seen.

Just as the crisis started to unfold in South Africa, Desmond and Leah began a three-month sabbatical at General Theological Seminary in New York City. Within six weeks of his arrival, Tutu received news that would change his life forever. On October 15, 1984, the Norwegian ambassador to the UN came to the Tutus' guest residence in Manhattan to inform them that Desmond would be awarded the Nobel Peace Prize, one of the world's highest honors. The announcement came just eight days after Tutu's 53rd birthday. The prize was awarded annually by a Norwegian-based committee to recognize an individual deemed to have done the most to promote peace in the world. Only one South African had ever been awarded the prize before—Albert Lutuli, president of the ANC, in 1960. Other past winners included Martin Luther King Jr. (1964) and Mother Teresa (1979). Tutu had been nominated for the prize twice before, in 1981 and 1982. The Nobel committee noted that the 1984 prize was for Tutu and all those in South Africa who were committed to "human dignity, fraternity, and democracy."[9]

The whole campus gathered at the seminary's chapel to celebrate the announcement of Tutu's award. As he entered the chapel, the crowd gave him a round of thunderous applause. Tutu said all black South Africans should know that the award acknowledged the just nature of their cause and that justice would prevail. Calls came in from all over the world to congratulate him. When word reached the SACC headquarters in Johannesburg, staff members sang and danced in the hallways. Those sending their congratulations included Mangosuthu Buthelezi, the chief minister of the KwaZulu homeland; ANC president Oliver Tambo; white opposition leader Frederick van zyl Slabbert; his colleague Helen Suzman; Pope John Paul II; 1983 Nobel Peace Prize winner Lech Walesa; Coretta Scott King; Ronald Reagan; Walter Mondale; Indira Gandhi; actress/activist Jane Fonda; and Nadine Gordimer, the famous South African writer. Even a senior South African security policeman congratulated Tutu. The Organization of African Unity, headquartered in Addis Ababa, Ethiopia, hailed the award as a signal of apartheid's impending demise.

Tutu wanted to return home immediately to celebrate the news with his fellow South Africans. He, his wife Leah, and their two daughters living in the United States flew first to London, where they were greeted and congratulated by the archbishop of Canterbury. During a news conference at Heathrow airport, Tutu said that most of his prize money (which totaled approximately $181,000) would go into a black South African educational fund.

The Tutus arrived back in South Africa on October 18, 1984. Hundreds of enthusiastic supporters met them at the Johannesburg airport, cheering, singing, and waving banners. The police ordered the crowd to disperse, and when this failed, they threatened to let their dogs loose on the people. Then "one of Tutu's associates pointed to the international television cameras and said, 'Please, feel free!'" Realizing they were faced with a no-win situation, the police kept their dogs at bay.[10]

At the SACC headquarters at Khotso House later that day, another crowd gathered for Tutu's arrival. An angry white man shouted abuse about Tutu and the award, but he couldn't spoil the festive atmosphere that prevailed. One black man told an SACC staffer that Tutu was a messiah who had come to liberate South Africa. After Tutu arrived, Rev. Allan Boesak and Rev. Beyers Naudé gave moving speeches congratulating their friend. Boesak, 15 years younger than Tutu, had also risen to prominence as a Christian critic of apartheid. A minister in the mixed-race branch of the Dutch Reformed Church, Boesak had become president of the World Alliance of Reformed Churches in 1982 and had played a key role in the establishment of the UDF in 1983. Naudé, an Afrikaner, had been stripped of his ministry by the DRC in the early 1960s for saying publicly that apartheid was unchristian. Shunned by his own people, he then formed the Christian Institute to mobilize church opposition to apartheid, but his work was cut short when both he and the institute were banned in 1977. During Tutu's formal welcome at Khotso House, Naudé looked over at his friend and said, "I pray to God that my people, the Afrikaner, will be able to change to such an extent that one day they will be able to see what a man of peace you really are."[11] Tutu thanked his supporters and said the prize was not his alone. It was for all South Africans who had struggled for freedom and dignity in South Africa, for those whose lives were torn apart by apartheid, for those who worked for peaceful change. He then led his colleagues in the hymn, "Let Us All Give Praise to the Lord."

Celebrations in Soweto followed. Tutu told his parishioners at St. Augustine's Church that the world recognized South Africa's freedom struggle. "Sometimes we may wonder if God loves us because we suffer in the land of our forefathers," he said. "Many a time we are tempted to lose faith in Him. And then God comes with a wonderful surprise. Just when our enemies begin to sing their victory songs, then God acts."[12] At a party later, Tutu told his friends not to put him on a pedestal. He and his wife needed their prayers as they faced their many responsibilities. If he "got too big for his boots," he said, his friends should tell him so.[13]

In contrast to the support Tutu received from the international community and his friends back home, the South African government reacted to the Nobel Prize announcement with a stony silence. Neither State President Botha nor any other government official formally congratulated Tutu on the award or offered any public comment. The state-run media at first buried news of Tutu's honor and then tried to discredit it. In one news broadcast, SABC television gave one minute of airtime to the Nobel Prize story, while devoting approximately 15 minutes to a rugby match. The report showed Tutu speaking but used a voice-over narration to imply that Tutu sought confrontation. He was shown gesturing wildly and then was quoted out of context to suggest that he wanted a bloodbath in South Africa. This was part of a long-running government campaign to discredit Tutu and distort his image. In its regular commentary on SABC radio, the government questioned whether Tutu met the criteria for the Nobel Prize. It suggested that the award "had degenerated into an international political instrument." Tutu's "contribution to peace in South Africa is neither remarkable nor consistent," said the commentator, adding that the bishop's utterances "have a ring of petulance."[14] The SABC's negative coverage did not go unanswered. Editors of the City Press, a black South

African newspaper, called the SABC's coverage of Tutu's prize a "scandalous and a despicable exhibition of gutter journalism."[15]

Criticism of Tutu's award was not just restricted to the government. Some white-owned South African newspapers criticized the award as well. The Afrikaans press was particularly incensed. Columns and editorials stressed that Tutu's radicalism and alleged advocacy of violence made him an unworthy recipient. Right-wing Christian groups in South Africa also criticized the announcement. Many white South Africans had long viewed Tutu with hostility, especially because of his calls for sanctions and his warnings of impending violence. These South Africans felt threatened by Tutu and were disgusted when the Nobel committee seemed to legitimize his views. Tutu had always been deeply troubled that white South Africans tended to demonize him, especially after his Nobel Prize was announced.

Not all commentary from the white-owned press was completely hostile. An editorial in the *Sunday Times*, one of South Africa's most widely read English newspapers, said that Tutu's award reflected the judgment of only a handful of Norwegians. But the paper recognized that the award bestowed prestige and moral authority upon its recipient. "We should pray that [Tutu] is granted great wisdom and courage in bearing his enhanced responsibility," the editors wrote.[16] Harald Pakendorf, the editor of the Afrikaans newspaper *Die Vaderland*, expressed mixed feelings. "The man says things that stick in one's craw and send blood rushing to one's head, yet he does talk of peace and he is a South African with status and authority," Pakendorf wrote.[17] He scolded the South African government for not formally congratulating Tutu on his award. So did Willem de Klerk, the editor of the Afrikaans Sunday newspaper *Rapport*. Longtime apartheid opponent and author Alan Paton congratulated Tutu for his prize but was troubled by Tutu's alleged advocacy of disinvestment (withdrawal of foreign investment) as a means to end apartheid. "I do not understand how you can put a man out of work for a high moral principle," he wrote.[18]

Tutu had not called for an end to all foreign investment in South Africa by this stage, but many interpreted his advocacy of foreign economic pressure as evidence that he favored complete disinvestment. This misunderstanding paralleled the widespread misconception in the white community that Tutu favored violence, when he actually warned against it. These distortions arose largely from the misleading propaganda that the government aired on South African radio and television. Amid all the praise and criticism, Tutu "sought to maintain his equilibrium on a seesaw of venom and jubilation."[19] At one point he was asked by a *Time* magazine correspondent to sum up his feelings about winning the Nobel Prize. "You feel humble, you feel proud, elated, and you feel sad," he said. "One of my greatest sadnesses is that there are many in this country who are not joining in celebrating something that is an honor for this country."[20]

Before Tutu returned to New York, another prominent South African clergyman gained attention—this time a white man. Peter Storey was the newly elected president of the Methodist Church of Southern Africa, and during his speech to the Methodist conference in Pretoria on October 20, 1984, he made a bold proposal. He called upon the South African liberation movements to lay down their arms and the government to unban them and invite them to talks about the country's future. Storey's proposal made headlines, but it was more than five years ahead of its time. Neither the government nor the liberation movements were ready to negotiate with each other yet, at least not publicly. Tutu endorsed the idea but said that black South Africans had little basis to trust the South African government. Still, Storey's speech showed that Tutu was not alone in his struggle against apartheid; there were other visionary South African Christians working for justice and peace at the same time.

Meanwhile, Tutu's Nobel Prize had transformed him into a celebrity. He was now indisputably the world's leading critic of apartheid. The South African government could not silence him, although they could still try to ignore or belittle him. Once he returned to the United States, he engaged in nonstop tours, speeches, press conferences, and interviews. He frequently appeared on TV news programs and talk shows. In fact, Tutu became so visible that Americans could not ignore him if they tried.

Shortly after arriving back in New York, Tutu was invited to address the UN Security Council. Now, to paraphrase Shakespeare, the world was Tutu's stage. In his speech on October 23, 1984, Tutu noted that South Africa had the potential to be the breadbasket of Africa, but despite its potential, it was a land of division and bitterness. "It is a highly volatile land," Tutu told the delegates, "and its inhabitants sit on a powder keg with a very short fuse indeed, ready to blow us all up into kingdom-come." He noted that the varied responses to his Nobel Prize reflected his country's deep divisions. He commended P. W. Botha for acknowledging that South Africa could no longer be governed by whites only, but the fatal flaw in the new constitution was that it excluded the African majority. The pillars of apartheid remained untouched, including the policy of depriving blacks of their South African citizenship. As Tutu put it, "Here I am, 53 years old, a bishop in the church, some would say reasonably responsible; I travel on a document that says of my nationality that it is 'undeterminable at present.'" He appealed to white South Africans to help build a new society and deplored violence from all quarters. He closed by asking the Security Council to pressure the South African government to begin negotiations with representatives of all sections of the population for a new, more just society. "I say we will all be free, and we ask you: help us, that this freedom comes for all of us in South Africa, black and white, but that it comes with the least possible violence, that it comes peacefully, that it comes soon," he said.[21]

Tutu's Nobel Peace Prize greatly inspired the antiapartheid movement in the United States. About six weeks after his award was announced, TransAfrica, a lobbying group on African and Caribbean affairs, launched a series of well-publicized protests in front of the South African embassy in Washington, D.C. TransAfrica's leader was Randall Robinson, an African American lawyer originally from Richmond, Virginia. He and his supporters organized the Free South Africa Movement, which not only coordinated the embassy protests but also urged the U.S. government to impose sanctions against South Africa. Suddenly, the combination of Tutu's presence in the United States, the protests at the South African embassy, and scenes of South African racial unrest on the nightly news made South Africa a highly visible, emotional news story in the United States.

The Nobel Prize not only guaranteed Tutu an audience with the American public, it also gave him access to key sectors of the U.S. government. In December 1984, Tutu met with the Congressional Black Caucus and the subcommittees on Africa in the House of Representatives and the Senate. His message was simple: although the South African government seemed to be undertaking reforms, apartheid still existed. "We don't want our chains comfortable," Tutu said. "We want them removed."[22] He told the House subcommittee on Africa that constructive engagement had been totally ineffective. He believed that the policy had emboldened the South African government to become more repressive because it thought it had the backing of powerful friends. Not one to mince words, Tutu labeled constructive engagement "immoral, evil, and totally unchristian." The subcommittee gave Tutu a standing ovation.[23]

Three days after testifying before the House subcommittee on Africa, Tutu was invited to the White House for a meeting with President Reagan. Reagan lacked an in-depth knowledge of South African affairs and viewed the South African government as a key anticommunist ally. He believed that P. W. Botha's government was moving in the right direction. Even though it was unlikely that Reagan would be swayed by Tutu's arguments, the latter's Nobel Prize made him too prestigious a figure to ignore. During their meeting in the Oval Office on December 7, 1984, Tutu strongly criticized the administration's policy of constructive engagement. He tried to convince the president that the situation in South Africa was deteriorating, but Reagan seemed unmoved. He defended his policy of quiet diplomacy toward South Africa and expressed his opposition to sanctions. The two parted cordially but remained far apart on U.S. policy toward South Africa. At a press conference after the meeting, Reagan insisted that the United States had succeeded in pressuring the South African government to move away from apartheid. Although Tutu obviously hadn't changed the president's mind, he was glad the meeting occurred, for he believed it would boost the morale of the antiapartheid movement back home. After all, the Reagan administration had not invited P. W. Botha to the White House—and it never would.

Despite his setback at the Oval Office, Tutu did not lose his sense of humor. Before he left for the Nobel Prize ceremony in Oslo, Norway, he spoke at the Waldorf-Astoria Hotel in New York City and told one of his favorite stories. "When the missionaries first came to Africa, they had the Bible and we had the land. They said, 'Let us pray.' We closed our eyes. When we opened them, we had the Bible and they had the land." Later he turned serious and called constructive engagement "an abomination, an unmitigated disaster."[24]

But perhaps Tutu's meeting with the president had more of an impact than he thought. Within a few weeks of Tutu's visit to the White House, Reagan issued his first substantive statement on South Africa. In uncharacteristically strong language, the president called for an end to forced removals and an end to detention without trial in South Africa. Clearly Reagan's advisers wanted to correct the impression that the president was too sympathetic toward Pretoria. The administration recognized that it could ill-afford to ignore the growing antiapartheid movement in the United States—or Desmond Tutu.

Soon it was time for Tutu to head to Oslo to accept the Nobel Prize. He brought an unusually large delegation (approximately 40 people) to accompany him. His delegation included Terry Waite, the archbishop of Canterbury's special envoy; the dean of the General Theological Seminary in New York; and a number of his coworkers from the South African Council of Churches. Assembling such an entourage was Tutu's way of thanking others and saying that the prize wasn't his alone. One SACC staffer who came to Oslo was amazed at all of the adoration Tutu received. He signed autographs and received VIP treatment from everyone he encountered. The festivities honoring Tutu included a torchlight parade through the streets of Oslo, a folk music concert, a state dinner, and an orchestral performance. During his stay in Norway, Tutu impressed people with his humility and gratitude. He was immensely proud of the award yet realized he was accepting it on behalf of his people.

At the formal award ceremony on December 10, 1984, Tutu wore a red cassock and a gold pectoral cross. The Norwegian chairman of the Nobel committee, Egil Aarvik, praised Tutu for leading the antiapartheid movement "with the weapons of the spirit and reason." The award recognized the courage of all South Africans who struggled against apartheid nonviolently, but it also recognized the unique role of Tutu himself. "Although he has never learned to hate, no one has opposed injustice with a more burning anger," said Aarvik. The Nobel committee hoped that the South African government would accept the olive branch from Tutu and others while there was still time. Regarding Tutu, Aarvik concluded, "With his warmhearted Christian faith he is a representative of the best in us all."[25] He then formally presented Tutu with a gold medal and his Nobel diploma.

In his brief acceptance statement, Tutu predicted that his award would kindle hope in the hearts of all those who were oppressed, whether in South Africa or the wider world. He told the audience,

> On behalf of all those for whom you have given new hope, a new cause for joy, I want to accept this award in a wholly representative capacity. I accept this prestigious award on behalf of my family, on behalf of the South African Council of Churches, on behalf of all in my motherland, on behalf of those committed to the cause of justice, peace, and reconciliation everywhere. If God be for us, who can be against us?[26]

During the formal award dinner, a bomb threat cleared the hall in which the guests were seated. Undaunted, Tutu led the guests in singing "We Shall Overcome" as they waited outside for police to check the hall. No bomb was ever found.

Tutu gave his formal Nobel lecture at the Oslo cathedral on December 11, 1984. He used the occasion to tell the world about apartheid in vivid, moving terms. He began by surveying the personal tragedies caused by apartheid in a land that claimed to be Christian. He noted how blacks were still being deported to homelands against their will, causing widespread starvation, especially among children. "Apartheid has ensured that God's children, just because they are black, should be treated as if they were things, and not as of infinite value as being created in the image of God," he said. He also described the costs of migrant labor, Bantu education, and detention without trial. Then he told this story: "Once a Zambian and a South African were talking. The Zambian boasted about their minister of naval affairs. The South African asked, 'But you have no navy, no access to the sea. How then can you have a Minister of Naval Affairs?' The Zambian retorted, 'Well, in South Africa you have a Minister of Justice, don't you?'" The anecdote was vintage Tutu. He skillfully used humor to win his audience over, but he also underscored an important point—that justice in South Africa was still elusive. He predicted that unrest would continue in South Africa until apartheid was completely dismantled. Once justice was given to all South Africans, regardless of race, then peace would prevail. Toward the end of his address, Tutu emphasized that all of the world's people deserved basic human rights, not just black South Africans, because all people were children of God. "God calls us to be his fellow workers with Him," he concluded, "so that we can extend his kingdom of shalom, of justice, of goodness, of compassion, of caring, of sharing, of laughter, joy, and reconciliation, so that the kingdom of this world will become the kingdom of our God and of His Christ, and He shall reign forever and ever. Amen."[27]

During his many travels as general secretary of the South African Council of Churches, Tutu had raised the world's consciousness about apartheid and urged the world to help end it. His charisma, eloquence, and quick wit made him the perfect spokesman for the black South African cause. His position as a bishop and a Nobel laureate elevated his status even further. By 1984, Tutu was the personification of the South African freedom struggle. But despite his stature as an international icon, the goals for which Tutu stood—justice, peace, and reconciliation in the land of his birth—still seemed beyond reach.

NOTES

1. Quoted in Shirley du Boulay, *Tutu: Voice of the Voiceless* (Grand Rapids, MI: William B. Eerdmans, 1988), p. 157.

2. Quoted in Robert Kinloch Massie, *Loosing the Bonds: The United States and South Africa in the Apartheid Years* (New York: Nan A. Talese, 1997), p. 513.

3. Quoted in Massie, *Loosing the Bonds,* p. 554.

4. Quoted in du Boulay, *Tutu,* p. 192.

5. Chester A. Crocker, *High Noon in Southern Africa: Making Peace in a Rough Neighborhood* (New York: W.W. Norton, 1992), p. 258.

6. Quoted in du Boulay, *Tutu,* p. 192.

7. Quoted in du Boulay, *Tutu,* pp. 197–98.

8. Desmond Tutu, *The Rainbow People of God: The Making of a Peaceful Revolution,* ed. John Allen (New York: Doubleday, 1994), pp. 82, 84.

9. Quoted in du Boulay, *Tutu,* p. 205.

10. Massie, *Loosing the Bonds*, p. 555.

11. J. P. H. Serfontein, "Reaction: The First Week—Day by Day," *Ecunews* 8 (December 1984): p. 8.

12. Chris More, "October 22—Satisfied Tutu Back to USA," *Ecunews* 8 (December 1984): pp. 10–11. Originally published in the *Star*, 22 October 1984.

13. Geoffrey Davies, "Tutu—The Man I Know," *Ecunews* 8 (December 1984): p. 15.

14. "SABC on the Nobel Prize," *Ecunews* 8 (December 1984): p. 8.

15. Serfontein, "Reaction," p. 9.

16. "The Name of the Prize is PEACE," *Sunday Times* (South Africa), 21 October 1984.

17. Harald Pakendorf, "The Wrong Time for Hoorays (and for Boos)," *Sunday Times*, 21 October 1984.

18. Alan Paton, "Paton on Tutu," *Sunday Times*, 21 October 1984.

19. Du Boulay, *Tutu*, p. 204.

20. "Searching for New Worlds," *Time*, 29 October 1984, p. 80.

21. Desmond Tutu, "The Question of South Africa," (address to the UN Security Council, 23 October 1984) in *The Global Experience: Readings in World History Since 1550*, ed. Philip Riley and others, vol. 2, 4th ed. (Upper Saddle River, NJ: Prentice Hall, 2002), pp. 312–14.

22. "Fresh Anger over Apartheid," *Time*, 17 December 1984, p. 46.

23. "Fresh Anger over Apartheid," p. 46.

24. "Fresh Anger over Apartheid," p. 46.

25. Egil Aarvik, "Presentation of the Nobel Peace Prize," (Oslo, Norway, 10 December 1984) in *Statements: Occasional Papers of the Phelps-Stokes Fund*, no. 1, November 1986, pp. 17–24.

26. Desmond Tutu, "Acceptance of the Nobel Peace Prize," (Oslo, Norway, 10 December 1984) in *Statements*, pp. 27–28.

27. Desmond Tutu, "Nobel Lecture," (Oslo, Norway, 11 December 1984) in *Statements*, pp. 31–39.

Chapter 11

BISHOP OF JOHANNESBURG

On November 13, 1984, Tutu was chosen to become the next bishop of Johannesburg, just one month after his Nobel Peace Prize was announced. He would become the first black ever to occupy the post, which was one of the highest in South Africa's Anglican Church. Tutu's selection had been controversial. Opponents suggested that he spent too much time outside of South Africa and that he was too ambitious and too political. Conservative whites tended to be the most skeptical; black priests the most enthusiastic. The Anglican elective assembly actually became dead-locked over the appointment of a new bishop. The synod of bishops intervened and chose Tutu after much deliberation.

Many black church leaders publicly praised Tutu's selection. Some prominent white church leaders did so as well, such as Archbishop of Cape Town Philip Russell and outgoing Bishop of Johannesburg Timothy Bavin. Other South Africans were less charitable. One homeland leader asked, "How can this man, preaching blood and starvation, call himself a Bishop in the Christian church?"[1] Conservative Christian organizations also criticized Tutu's selection. The leader of one such group blasted Tutu's appointment and predicted (quite wrongly) that "in a few years Bishop Tutu will probably be no more than a forgotten demagogue."[2] A former mayor of Johannesburg announced that he was leaving the Anglican Church because of Tutu's promotion. Former *Rand Daily Mail* editor Allister Sparks did the opposite. He publicly announced that he was rejoining the Anglican Church because Tutu was elected bishop of Johannesburg. In his eyes, Tutu's appointment signaled the church's willingness to face the problems in South Africa head on.

Before Tutu assumed his new position, he prepared to host a well-known American visitor—Senator Edward Kennedy of Massachusetts. Tutu and Allan Boesak had invited Kennedy to South Africa because they believed that his visit would help focus international attention on apartheid. Kennedy's eight-day stay in South Africa in January 1985 generated enormous controversy. Upon his arrival at the Johannesburg airport, Kennedy was warmly welcomed by Tutu, Boesak, and Beyers Naudé, who was chosen to replace Tutu as head of the South African Council of Churches. But Kennedy was jeered by members of the Azanian People's Organization (AZAPO), a prominent black consciousness group. They viewed Kennedy as a symbol of American capitalism and imperialism who had no business speaking on behalf of black South Africans. AZAPO supporters disrupted the senator's later engagements in the country, much to the delight of the South African government. The government accused Kennedy of trying to use South Africa to enhance his political popularity back home.

Kennedy's visit was scheduled to culminate in a speech at Soweto's Regina Mundi Church. As Tutu prepared to introduce his American guest, 100 AZAPO protesters stormed the church, waving anti-Kennedy signs and insisting that the senator leave. Visibly shaken, Tutu urged the crowd to let Kennedy speak. Troops and police surrounded the church, believing a major confrontation would occur. Although most of the 4,000 people in the hall wanted to hear the senator, the atmosphere became too tense. Tutu and Kennedy agreed that the speech had to be cancelled before more serious trouble broke out. Kennedy left without addressing the crowd and went straight to the airport. Tutu was terribly embarrassed that his friend had been shouted down. From then on, he distanced himself from the black consciousness movement and moved closer to the multiracial United Democratic Front.

AZAPO wasn't the only force in black South African politics with which Tutu clashed. Another was Mangosuthu Buthelezi, one of South Africa's most highly visible black leaders in the 1980s. Buthelezi was chief minister of the KwaZulu homeland and leader of Inkatha, a Zulu cultural organization. He was both powerful and controversial. Some blacks (and whites) supported him because he criticized apartheid, called for the release of Nelson Mandela, and refused to accept independence for the KwaZulu homeland. But Buthelezi spoke out against school boycotts, sanctions, and disinvestment, strategies that many in the antiapartheid movement supported. He also opposed the ANC's armed struggle. Buthelezi enjoyed the support of many Zulu rural dwellers and hoped to establish a nationwide following.

Problems between Buthelezi and Tutu began in March 1978, during the funeral of Robert Sobukwe. Buthelezi was scheduled to address the mourners, but an angry crowd of young blacks chased him away, accusing him of being a collaborator with the apartheid regime. Tutu and others helped lead Buthelezi to safety. Later Tutu tried to calm the crowd down. Without condoning the youths' actions, he said that he understood their anger. Young black South Africans were beginning to reject fellow blacks who worked within government structures in the police, town councils, and the homelands. Buthelezi was deeply humiliated by the youths' actions and partly blamed Tutu for the events at the funeral. He frequently attacked Tutu in the months ahead. Animosity between the two men grew from then on.

The future, not the past, dominated Tutu's thoughts when he was enthroned as bishop of Johannesburg on Sunday, February 3, 1985. Two thousand guests packed St. Mary's Cathedral for the ceremony, over which Archbishop Russell presided. The service was both multilingual and multiracial, reflecting South Africa's diversity. Right-wing whites had made undisclosed threats against Tutu before the service, so security was tight. In his enthronement address, Tutu said that he hoped he would not be "quite such a horrible ogre" as some feared. He used humor once again to disarm his critics. Although he touched on political issues, his speech was not solely political. He criticized apartheid and promised to call for economic sanctions if apartheid wasn't dismantled in the next two years. He realized many whites were uncomfortable with his appointment, especially because they thought he promoted violence and communism. He reaffirmed his commitment to peaceful change but said pressure was needed to bring about such change. As for communism, he said he hated it "with every fiber of my being." Blacks sometimes accepted help from communists, he explained, because help from others was not forthcoming. "When you are in a dungeon and a hand is stretched out to free you, you do not ask for the pedigree of the hand owner," he said.

Tutu concentrated mostly on the role of the church in South Africa. He believed God called upon his followers to be peacemakers, no matter what the personal cost. God should be more than an object of worship on Sunday mornings. "He rejects as an utter abomination religious acts however meticulously carried out if they have no bearing on how the people live out their everyday lives outside Church." Tutu continued,

> Jesus says we will be judged whether we are fit for heaven or the warmer place, not by whether we prayed or went to church...but by whether we fed or did not feed the hungry, we

clothed or did not clothe the naked, we visited or did not visit the sick and the imprisoned.... The Bible says, love God, love your neighbor. It is two sides of the same coin. The coin must have both. Our love of God is authenticated and expressed in and through our love of neighbor.

Tutu concluded by pledging to love his flock deeply, even if they didn't all love him.[3]

The Anglican diocese of Johannesburg over which Tutu now presided was the largest in South Africa. It had 102 parishes and 300,000 Anglicans, approximately 80 percent of whom were black. Tutu familiarized himself with conditions in all of his parishes in the huge diocese. He already had the goodwill of the vast majority of his black parishioners; he sought to dispel fears in the white community by visiting their parishes as well. He wanted to soften his image as a fire-breathing radical. Some whites began to warm up to him, while others remained hostile. Some resented Tutu so much that they even refused to let him give their children communion.

While Tutu immersed himself in his new diocese, conditions in South Africa began to demand his immediate attention. The wave of protests that had begun in September 1984 had intensified. Troops patrolled the townships in increasing numbers, and police continued to use deadly force to crush demonstrators. During the first eight months of 1985, the government detained approximately 8,000 people, many of whom were under 18. Despite the police sweeps, violence only worsened. Murders of high-profile activists began to occur more frequently. A power struggle between the UDF and Inkatha became deadly. Township activists began targeting enemies in their midst, such as town councillors and police informers. They began to use a new method of execution on suspected collaborators—the "necklace." Activists would force an automobile tire around their victim's neck and shoulders, douse it with gasoline, ignite it, and watch as the person burned to death. Sometimes television crews were on hand to record the deadly spectacle.

Tutu was horrified by the escalation of violence from both sides. He tried to promote peaceful change amid a situation that was becoming more violent each day. Continuing to stress peace and nonviolence was not easy, especially when some blacks viewed violence as the only option left to resist apartheid. Young blacks in particular were losing patience with Tutu's moderation.

International news teams swarmed into South Africa to cover the escalating racial conflict. One of the most high-profile American programs to focus on South Africa in this period was *Nightline*, the ABC news program hosted by Ted Koppel. *Nightline* came to South Africa for a series of five broadcasts in March 1985. The South African government not only agreed to let the *Nightline* staff use its studios, it also agreed to broadcast the programs in South Africa 12 hours after they were shown in the United States. Bishop Tutu and Foreign Minister Pik Botha (no relation to State President P. W. Botha) were scheduled to appear on the first program on March 18, 1985. Tutu would be seated in a Johannesburg church, Botha in a studio in Cape Town. This was a historic event in television journalism. Not only had Tutu and Botha never publicly debated each other, but no South African government official had ever debated a black antiapartheid leader on television before. Foreign Minister Botha was a skilled debater determined to counteract the negative image of South Africa abroad. Tutu was quite nervous as he prepared for the broadcast. "I was very concerned that I could end up with a lot of egg on my face," he admitted later.[4]

With Ted Koppel moderating from Johannesburg, the discussion between Tutu and Botha began cordially but then became more heated. Tutu made an impassioned statement about the many injustices of apartheid, such as pass laws, migrant labor, and forced removals. He described apartheid "as evil as Communism and Nazism." When Botha bristled with an angry rebuttal, the fireworks began. At one point, Tutu noted that he couldn't vote in the land of his birth. Botha replied that Tutu had declined to vote in one of the "national states" (homelands) of which he was a part. Then Tutu interjected, "Excuse me! Excuse me!" but Botha continued. Clearly the two sides were still far apart, but at least they were talking. The men also debated the significance of government reforms and whether international pressure was needed to end apartheid.[5]

Afterward, Tutu was pleased that the debate had taken place because the government had long sought to avoid public discussions with blacks outside the system. The program was aired on SABC the next day and received a great deal of publicity. Although the government censored taped segments from ABC highlighting unrest and inequality in South Africa, they left the Tutu-Botha interchange intact. One Afrikaner journalist was greatly impressed by what he saw. He felt an important dialogue had begun between the government and the antiapartheid movement. "And the important thing was that Tutu was so human, so reasonable," he said. "It was certain that South Africans would watch this and wonder, 'Now what's so awful about at least talking with these people?'"[6]

Following the *Nightline* series, the American public became more interested in South Africa than ever before. The antiapartheid movement gained momentum at American colleges and universities during the spring of 1985. Some student groups, disturbed by news of worsening racial clashes in South Africa, began to urge their institutions to withdraw their investments from firms that operated in South Africa. In some cases students resorted to civil disobedience to make their point. At Columbia University in New York City, students blockaded an administration building for several weeks to demonstrate their support for disinvestment. When the administration threatened to expel them, Tutu sent a telegram welcoming the students' efforts. He undertook a speaking tour of the United States in May 1985 and was greatly heartened that American college students were organizing against apartheid. His itinerary included Harvard, UCLA, Berkeley, and the University of California at Davis. He was thrilled by what he encountered: "It was an incredible thing! Those students helped us recover our faith in humanity. They should have been busy with their final exams and worrying about grades. But at Davis there were 15,000 of them sitting in the sun, waiting for me to speak. Incredible. Incredible."[7] By the end of spring, some American colleges and church denominations had begun to disinvest, as had various state and local governments.

Meanwhile, the situation in South Africa continued to deteriorate. As more blacks lost their lives in political violence, funerals became ever more frequent. Mass burials were transformed into political rallies as mourners sang liberation songs and rededicated themselves to the freedom struggle. Passions often ran high at these funerals, as Tutu quickly discovered.

One particularly tense funeral at which Tutu spoke was held in Duduza, a township east of Johannesburg. It had become a center of protest and violence by mid-1985. In July, Tutu presided at the funeral of four men suspected of having been killed by the police. As the funeral proceeded, the crowd suddenly attacked an onlooker whom they accused of being a police spy. Tutu pleaded with the mourners to let the man go, but they ignored him. Fearing that the man was about to be killed, Tutu and another African priest plunged into the crowd and dragged the injured man to a car that took him to the hospital. Without the intervention of Tutu and his colleague, the man certainly would have been killed. A few days later, Duduza residents attacked another suspected informer, but this time Tutu wasn't there to intervene. A woman was beaten, stoned, and burned to death by an angry crowd while TV cameras recorded the whole grisly scene.

At a funeral later that week in KwaThema, another township east of Johannesburg, Tutu condemned the murder in Duduza. Addressing 30,000 people at the KwaThema stadium, he said,

I understand when people are angry or hurt and want to take it out on those we think are collaborators. But I abhor all forms of violence. I want to condemn in the strongest possible terms what happened in Duduza. Many of our supporters around the world said then 'Oh, oh. If they do those things maybe they are not ready for freedom.' Let us demonstrate the discipline of people who know that they are ready for freedom. At the end of the day we must be able to walk with our heads high.... If you do that kind of thing again, I will find it difficult to speak for the cause of liberation. If the violence continues, I will pack my bags, collect my family and leave this beautiful country that I love so passionately.[8]

Tutu's comments showed that he abhorred not just government-sponsored violence, but all violence. By criticizing black South Africans whose cause he championed, he risked losing support, but he spoke out nevertheless.

When word spread that Tutu had threatened to leave South Africa if the violence didn't stop, some young blacks said "Good! Good riddance" because they saw him as standing in the way of their revolution.[9] One young mixed-race woman in Johannesburg described Tutu as "too moderate for most of us, too much within the system. The old respect for authority is dying out, and Tutu represents that authority."[10] Remarks like this highlighted the rising tide of black anger in South Africa. Many victims of apartheid had had enough of talking; their elders had tried that for years and had gotten nowhere. Tutu understood the impatience of black South African youth. According to one journalist, Tutu even admitted that "if he were a young black, he wouldn't follow a man named Bishop Tutu."[11] Tutu's dilemma was clear. Hated by many white South Africans for being too radical, he was also scorned by many black militants for being too moderate.

Soon the atmosphere in South Africa became even more polarized. On July 20, 1985, the government declared a state of emergency in parts of the country most affected by unrest. The state of emergency gave police wide new powers to act against perceived threats. It also restricted the rights of detainees and the press and limited public gatherings. Police began a massive roundup of suspected activists, many of whom were detained without being put on trial. The government's crackdown signaled that South Africa had entered the most serious crisis in its history.

Just after the state of emergency was declared, Tutu sent an urgent telegram to State President P. W. Botha requesting a meeting. Botha refused, saying that Tutu had not renounced violence or civil disobedience. Botha did agree to meet a small church delegation in August, but he would not meet Tutu individually. Angered by Botha's refusal to meet with him, Tutu told journalists, "The youth are right, and we have nothing to show for the advocacy of nonviolence except the continued intransigence of the government and an escalation of their own violence. I have tried, and I have failed."[12] As if Botha's snub weren't enough, Tutu's son, Trevor, was detained for 14 days in August 1985 for swearing at a policeman. As Bishop Tutu observed later, "This government believes when people get obstreperous, why, just boink them one on the head and you will have sorted them out properly."[13]

A month into the state of emergency, the government hinted that P. W. Botha would announce major reforms in a speech to the party faithful. Expectations soared, particularly overseas. But in an angry and defiant speech, Botha lashed out at the rest of the world for pressuring South Africa and failed to announce any significant changes. He even suggested that his government might use stronger measures to crack down on its opponents. Botha's bluster alienated many in the outside world and paved the way for intensified international pressure. Tutu was so disappointed by Botha's speech that he began to consider calling for punitive sanctions sooner than he had originally planned. "Short of a miracle, short of decisive intervention by the international community, we are for the birds," he said. He believed Botha wanted to use military force to "bludgeon blacks into total submission."[14]

Tutu's mood became increasingly grim during this period, amid the state of emergency, Botha's speech, rising black anger, and police provocation. Despite his feelings of despair, he still believed that God would intervene. He insisted that he would continue to try to talk with the government, even though many in the black community thought such efforts were a waste of time. Tutu told *Time* magazine,

> I am not a politician. My paradigm comes from the Scriptures. I say to the government that it cannot prescribe to me what I preach. Equally, no one in the black community can prescribe to me what I should do.... I have to follow biblical paradigms; prophets go on talking to kings; Moses goes to Pharaoh, even when he is told that Pharaoh is going to harden his heart. But he goes.[15]

Tutu finally received some welcome news in September 1985. Under pressure from Congress, the Reagan administration approved a package of mild sanctions against South Africa. It banned U.S. loans to the South African government, banned the importation of Krugerrands (South African gold coins), banned the sale of nuclear technology and computers to the South African government, and banned arms deals between the United States and South Africa. Tutu was heartened that Congress had pressured the White House to act. He saw it as a sign that the world was increasingly willing to take action against apartheid. The imposition of American sanctions was due to a variety of factors: outrage over Botha's speech; continued repression inside South Africa and military aggression beyond its borders; and the efforts of the Congressional Black Caucus, TransAfrica, university students, and others. These developments, combined with Tutu's urgings, had strengthened the case for sanctions, at least in the eyes of key American lawmakers.

Tutu believed the time had come to push for even tougher measures. He took to the skies again in October 1985. During a stop in London, he tried in vain to convince British Prime Minister Margaret Thatcher to take a harder line against South Africa. Thatcher believed that Botha's government had embarked upon major reforms, whereas Tutu dismissed these steps out of hand. "Anyone who thinks we should rejoice because the Immorality Act [banning interracial sex] has been properly amended is like someone who wants you to celebrate because some guy no longer beats his wife. Why should we be thrilled when it was the government itself who established all of these obnoxious laws in the first place?"[16] Tutu also addressed the political committee of the UN General Assembly in New York. He told the committee members that life for black South Africans was getting worse, not better. Not only were large numbers of black South Africans losing their lives, but peaceful protest was all but impossible. He said that if apartheid was not dismantled within six months, the world should apply punitive economic sanctions. "Let us be part of the exhilarating enterprise of liberating South Africa for all its people, black and white together," he concluded.[17]

During his stay in the United States, Tutu announced the creation of the Bishop Tutu Scholarship Fund. This would help pay the college expenses of black South Africans in exile. It was especially designed to help students enroll in U.S. colleges and universities so they could develop skills needed back home. Tutu hoped to raise one million dollars for the fund before he returned to South Africa. He also made a substantial donation of his own to the fund.

As Tutu traveled back and forth between South Africa and foreign destinations, white South African hostility toward him grew. He was regularly criticized in the white press and received more threats and harassing phone calls. Despite the threats, Tutu took only minimal security precautions. His office windows were made of one-way glass and his car had darkened windows. Beyond that, Tutu hoped his faith in God and his international visibility would protect him from harm. He kept his sense of humor amid the escalating personal attacks. He asked two visiting American journalists, "Have you heard the latest story they're telling about me? There's a new Kentucky Fried Tutu. You know what it's got? Two left wings and a parson's nose!"[18] Sometimes white hostility toward Tutu eased when people heard him speak in person. This was the case when Tutu preached at an Anglican Church in Rosebank, a wealthy white Johannesburg suburb, in 1985. Instead of haranguing the congregation with angry accusations, he "approached the congregation with gentle humor, acknowledging that he was not particularly welcome in that parish." He then gave a sermon on love and reconciliation. Some of the whites left the church with considerably less hostility than they had had when they arrived.[19]

Tutu took an 18-day trip to the United States in January 1986. He wanted to discuss the deteriorating situation in his country and to urge Americans to back tougher measures against the South African government. His stops included New York, Washington, D.C., Baltimore, Philadelphia, Chicago, Detroit, Atlanta, Los Angeles, San Diego, and the San Francisco Bay Area. Often he gave several speeches a day. During his visit to Detroit, Tutu met with the chairmen of General Motors and Burroughs Corporation, both of which had major operations in South Africa. He also spoke to the Detroit Economic Club. He urged businessmen to set a deadline for South Africa. Either specific progress should be made by a certain date—such as lifting the state of emergency, pulling troops out of the townships, releasing political prisoners—or American businesses should pull out of the country entirely.

On January 20, 1986, Tutu was awarded the Martin Luther King Jr. Peace Prize at King's old church in Atlanta, Ebenezer Baptist Church. King's widow, Coretta Scott King, hailed Tutu as a man who "speaks with the moral authority, courage, and vision that distinguished Martin Luther King Jr."[20] Later that day Tutu flew to Los Angeles, where he participated in ceremonies honoring the first observance of the Martin Luther King holiday. He paid tribute to King for his inspiration and thanked the American people for urging their government to put pressure on South Africa. While in Los Angeles, Tutu was asked a question about comparisons between himself and Martin Luther King Jr. "I have said that I do not belong in the same league with Dr. Martin Luther King Jr.," Tutu replied. "I am not being falsely modest. He was an outstanding person who was an original thinker. He was a pacifist, which I am not. I am a peace-lover."[21] Although Tutu was dedicated to nonviolence, he could understand why some people resorted to violence if they had exhausted all other alternatives. At one point during his U.S. visit, Tutu warned that unless apartheid was dismantled soon, blacks might attack white schoolchildren or poison the coffee of their white employers. That remark stirred up great anger among white South Africans, as if he were advocating such action. He was not. Rather, he was warning about the potentially deadly consequences of black anger if repression continued.

Tutu's warnings about black anger and his threat to endorse sanctions set off a firestorm of controversy in South Africa—at least among many whites. SABC radio accused Tutu of encouraging further violence with his remarks. Many whites called for the government to prosecute Tutu, but the government decided not to, fearing that such action would only make Tutu a martyr. Some angry white Anglicans believed Tutu was raising money in the United States to support the armed liberation movement. Others suggested that he be expelled from the church and even arrested. A number of white Anglicans boycotted church after Tutu returned to South Africa; others withdrew their financial support. Editors of the progovernment newspaper The Citizen wrote, "There is no greater thorn in South Africa's side than this man of the cloth who strides through the world like a religious pop star."[22]

Despite the controversy his latest trip had generated, Tutu still viewed himself as a peacemaker. He tried to defuse a potentially volatile situation in the Johannesburg township of Alexandra in February 1986. The residents' anger was about to boil over due to recent clashes with the police, in which 19 people had been killed. In response, residents set buildings on fire and placed barricades on the streets to block police vehicles. Tutu urged the people to be patient and nonviolent. Assuring them that God was on their side, he promised to present the residents' demands (withdrawal of the police, release of detainees, an end to the state of emergency) to State President Botha. Tutu traveled to Cape Town, but Botha refused to see him. Tutu was only able to see Deputy Minister of Law and Order Adrian Vlok, who refused to accede to the demands of Alexandra residents. Tutu's efforts had gotten nowhere. He reported back to 40,000 people at the Alexandra stadium upon his return to the Johannesburg area. Again he pleaded for patience, but this time he was booed. The crowd's anger signaled that time was running out for relatively peaceful change. Tutu was in danger of becoming marginalized; neither the government nor black militants seemed to be listening to him.

It was against this background that Tutu formally asked the international community to impose sanctions on South Africa. In the statement he issued from Johannesburg on April 2, 1986, he noted that more than 1,200 blacks had been killed in political unrest since August 1984. He felt that only outside pressure could save the country. Although Tutu's call for sanctions was technically illegal, he was not arrested. His international standing had protected him once again. Many critics of sanctions argued that they would increase unemployment and thus hurt black South Africans the most. Tutu rejected this argument. People who expressed this idea, he said, were displaying a sudden concern for blacks that was rather curious, given their past behavior. When a government minister criticized Tutu's stand on sanctions because it would allegedly lead to black suffering, Tutu responded, "His new found altruism is quite galling, when you realize that he is a member of a government whose policies have inflicted quite deliberately...unnecessary and unacceptable suffering on our people. The minister should spare us his crocodile tears."[23]

Tutu returned to the United States in May 1986 to generate support for international sanctions. He criticized the British and American governments for not intervening more decisively on behalf of black South Africans and suggested the story would be different if the victims were white. During a stop in Toronto in early June, Tutu said that if sanctions didn't work, "the Church would have no alternative but to say it would be justifiable to use violence and force to overthrow an unjust regime."[24] He had never before come so close to endorsing armed resistance. But he had not yet given up on nonviolence. He and TransAfrica director Randall Robinson cooperated in a nationwide direct mail campaign to solicit support for the Free South Africa Movement in the United States, which was coordinating protests at the South African embassy in Washington and pressuring the American government to impose harsher sanctions on South Africa.

Shortly after Tutu returned to South Africa in mid-June 1986, the government imposed a new, nationwide state of emergency to head off protests marking the 10th anniversary of the Soweto uprising. All such commemorations were banned—even church services. In a massive security sweep in the days before June 16, police arrested 2,000 people. Tutu condemned the arrests and vowed to defy the ban on events marking the Soweto anniversary. On June 13, the day after the new state of emergency was declared, Tutu met with P. W. Botha for 90 minutes in Cape Town. This was the two men's first meeting in six years. Botha expressed confidence in his government's ability to restore law and order; Tutu argued that law and order based on injustice could not last indefinitely. The meeting achieved little, but Tutu had risked his credibility among black groups by meeting with Botha at all.

Tutu was determined to preach the gospel, despite the new restrictions on church services. On Sunday, June 15, 1986, Tutu led an outdoor church service in Evaton, a black township south of Johannesburg. The mood was somber for several reasons. Not only were people mindful of the Soweto anniversary and the new state of emergency, but they had also learned that five Anglican ministers had recently been detained under the emergency regulations. Tutu told the worshippers, "The problems of our country aren't going to be solved by locking up leaders like this. Not by petrol bombs, not by children being shot. Our problems will be solved when we sit and negotiate.... We don't want to oppress anyone, to drive anyone into the sea. We only want what white people want for themselves."[25] Tutu prayed for those killed 10 years earlier and assured the crowd that one day they would be free. As he spoke, soldiers and police vehicles began to congregate ominously near the church. Fearing police retaliation, the black worshippers hesitated to leave church property once the service ended. Tutu and Leah then strode hand in hand toward the gate and motioned for people to come forward. Slowly they did, shaking Tutu's hand as they filed out and crossed the police gauntlet. Once again Tutu had defused a potentially volatile situation.

On Monday, June 16, 1986, troops streamed into Soweto to enforce the ban on commemorations and rallies. They guarded entrances to the township and set up roadblocks, while the government cut off telephone service to Soweto. This was all part of an extraordinary effort to intimidate residents and avoid a repeat of the June 1976 protests. As Tutu was driving to Johannesburg on the morning of the 16th, he was stopped at three roadblocks and searched twice. "It doesn't matter if you're a Bishop of one of the most important dioceses in this province, it doesn't matter if you're a Nobel Peace Prize winner in this country. What matters is you're black," Tutu said. "That is good for Tutu to remember."[26] Later that day, Tutu led a service at St. Mary's Cathedral in central Johannesburg. He also issued a plea for intensified sanctions that was prominently published in the *New York Times*. "There is no room for neutrality," he wrote. "Are you on the side of oppression or liberation? Are you on the side of death or life? Are you on the side of goodness or evil?"[27]

P. W. Botha agreed to meet with Tutu again in July, perhaps believing that it would improve his government's international image. He had no intention of taking Tutu's requests seriously. During their two-hour meeting on July 21, 1986, Tutu urged the state president to lift the emergency, but Botha said this would lead to more violence. He also warned Tutu to stop calling for international sanctions against South Africa. Under the state of emergency, making such calls was considered a crime and could result in 10 years in prison. Tutu pressed Botha to unban the ANC and begin negotiations on South Africa's future with the people's authentic leaders. Botha insisted that he would negotiate only with those who renounced violence. He would not abandon his hard-line stance, so the stalemate continued.

Meanwhile, in the United States, President Reagan faced growing pressure from Congress to intensify sanctions against South Africa. In a speech he gave on July 22, 1986, Reagan reaffirmed his opposition to such a move. Apartheid was wrong and unacceptable, he admitted, but he praised the South African government for the dramatic changes it had introduced. In his view, Pretoria (the administrative capital) was under no obligation to negotiate with organizations that promoted terrorism or communism. Dismissing the idea of imposing further sanctions, Reagan said that the West should strengthen its economic ties to South Africa. He also suggested that black South Africans bore a heavy responsibility for the violence in their country.[28]

South African Foreign Minister Pik Botha warmly welcomed Reagan's stand. He viewed it as an official endorsement of his government's approach. Tutu, on the other hand, found the president's statement "utterly racist and totally disgusting.... The West, as far as I am concerned, can go to Hell," he said.[29] Although Tutu genuinely liked Americans, he was often dismayed by American foreign policy. He was not the only one critical of Reagan's speech. So was Republican Senator Richard Lugar, the chairman of the Senate Foreign Relations Committee. So were many other members of Congress. Even Reagan's assistant secretary of state for African affairs, Chester Crocker, was taken aback by Reagan's "strident pro-Pretoria tilt."[30]

Soon Tutu was on the move again, this time to Japan, China, and Jamaica in August 1986. He repeated his calls for economic sanctions. One official from the South African government commented that Tutu's remarks bordered on high treason. Whites intensified their calls for Tutu to be silenced. Despite the animosity, Tutu remained determined to rally the world against apartheid. But his stormy tenure as bishop of Johannesburg was about to end—it was time for him to answer an even higher calling.

NOTES

1. Shirley du Boulay, *Tutu: Voice of the Voiceless* (Grand Rapids, MI: William B. Eerdmans, 1988), p. 211.

2. "What They Said," *Ecunews* 8 (December 1984): p. 5.

3. Desmond Tutu, "One Holy Catholic and Apostolic Church," *Ecunews* 9 (January–February 1985): pp. 29–36.

4. Ted Koppel and Kyle Gibson, *Nightline: History in the Making and the Making of Television* (New York: Times Books, 1996), p. 66.

5. *Nightline* broadcast, ABC, 18 March 1985.

6. Quoted in Koppel and Gibson, *Nightline*, p. 82.

7. Marc Cooper and Greg Goldin, "An Interview with Bishop Desmond Tutu," in *South Africa: Apartheid and Disinvestment, The Reference Shelf*, ed. Steven Anzovin (New York: H.W. Wilson Company, 1987), 59, pp. 108–25. Originally published in *Rolling Stone*, 21 November 1985.

8. Steven Mufson, *Fighting Years: Black Resistance and the Struggle for a New South Africa* (Boston: Beacon Press, 1990), p. 99 and du Boulay, *Tutu*, p. 223.

9. Cooper and Goldin, "An Interview with Bishop Desmond Tutu," p. 122.

10. Carolyn Meyer, *Voices of South Africa: Growing Up in a Troubled Land* (San Diego: Harcourt Brace Jovanovich, 1986), p. 202.

11. Mufson, *Fighting Years*, p. 103.

12. "South Africa Snubs Tutu, May Oust Foreign Workers," *Chicago Tribune*, 30 July 1985.

13. Cooper and Goldin, "An Interview with Bishop Desmond Tutu," p. 117.

14. "Bishop Tutu Sees a 'Catastrophe' for South Africa," *New York Times*, 17 August 1985.

15. "Bishop Tutu's Hopes and Fears," *Time*, August 19, 1985, p. 26.

16. Cooper and Goldin, "An Interview with Bishop Desmond Tutu," p. 120.

17. Desmond Tutu, *The Rainbow People of God: The Making of a Peaceful Revolution*, ed. John Allen (New York: Doubleday, 1994), p. 103.

18. Cooper and Goldin, "An Interview with Bishop Desmond Tutu," p. 108.

19. Meyer, *Voices of South Africa*, p. 196.

20. "Tutu Praises US Public's Role in Forcing Action Against Apartheid," *Los Angeles Times*, 21 January 1986.

21. "Tutu Praises U.S. Public's Role."

22. Robert Kinloch Massie, *Loosing the Bonds: The United States and South Africa in the Apartheid Years* (New York: Nan A. Talese, 1997), p. 612.

23. Du Boulay, *Tutu*, p. 242.

24. Quoted in du Boulay, *Tutu*, p. 243.

25. "Bishop Tutu Presses Case for Freedom as Tension in South Africa Continues," *Wall Street Journal*, 16 June 1986.

26. Mufson, *Fighting Years*, p. 264.

27. Massie, *Loosing the Bonds*, p. 613.

28. "Sanctions Would Backfire—Reagan," *Los Angeles Times*, 23 July 1986 and Massie, *Loosing the Bonds*, pp. 615–16.

29. "'West Can Go to Hell,' Angry Tutu Replies," *Los Angeles Times*, 23 July 1986.

30. Chester A. Crocker, *High Noon in Southern Africa: Making Peace in a Rough Neighborhood* (New York: W.W. Norton, 1992), p. 323.

Chapter 12

ARCHBISHOP OF CAPE TOWN

As Tutu finished his first year as bishop of Johannesburg, the leader of South Africa's Anglican Church, Philip Russell, announced his plan to retire as archbishop of Cape Town in August 1986. An Anglican advisory committee placed Tutu's name on the ballot to replace him. Tutu had also been nominated as a candidate for the position in 1981, but he had not received the necessary two-thirds majority in the election that followed. Tutu had not actively sought the appointment then or five years later when he was renominated. He planned to stay on as bishop of Johannesburg for the foreseeable future. His wife, Leah, had friends and a job in Johannesburg and was not eager to move. Some in the elective assembly feared that choosing Tutu might drive whites away from the church or further poison church-state relations in South Africa. But despite these reservations, Tutu was elected archbishop in April 1986, without the delays that had marred his appointment as bishop of Johannesburg. He would become the 11th archbishop of Cape Town and the first black in South African history to hold the position.

Reacting to his election, Tutu told the press, "I'm tongue-tied, and some people hope it's permanent. It's like a dream. I am overcome by the awesomeness of it all, and of the tremendous responsibility that has been placed on my shoulders."[1] His election was hailed by a diverse array of groups and individuals, including white liberal political organizations, AZAPO, the archbishop of Canterbury, Allan Boesak, and even Mangosuthu Buthelezi. Some newspapers greeted Tutu's election cautiously, hoping the appointment would somehow moderate his political activity. President Botha reacted to Tutu's election the same way he had to Tutu's

Nobel Peace Prize—with no comment. Conservative whites predictably criticized the selection, saying it would lead to greater racial tension. Anti-Tutu graffiti appeared in South Africa, such as, "I was an Anglican until I put Tu and Tu together." On a wall where an admirer had initially sprayed "God loves Tutu," someone added, "The Gods must be crazy." Although Tutu found this kind of graffiti amusing, he sometimes shuddered when he encountered hostility in person. "If looks could kill, they murdered me many times over," he said of his detractors. "When I got on a plane in Johannesburg or a train in Cape Town, the looks that I got were enough to curdle milk."[2]

Tutu invited friends from all over the world to attend his installation ceremony on September 7, 1986. Among the 1,700 guests who filed into St. George's Cathedral in Cape Town were archbishop of Canterbury Robert Runcie, Coretta Scott King, Winnie Mandela, Allan Boesak, Beyers Naudé, plus Tutu's wife, all four children, and his sister Gloria. The grand cathedral was filled with the sounds of both traditional hymns and African songs performed by a choir from Soweto. In his enthronement address, Tutu reiterated his favorite theme: if Christians profess to love God, they must also love their neighbor. He told his listeners, "If we could but recognize our common humanity, that we do belong together, that our destinies are bound up with another's, that we can be free only together, that we can survive only together, that we can be human only together, then a glorious South Africa would come into being where all of us lived harmoniously together as members of one family, God's family." Tutu's theology centered on the African concept of "ubuntu," meaning a person is a person through other persons. The concept stressed the interconnectedness of human society and the need for people to treat others as part of their extended human family. Tutu also emphasized the need for forgiveness in a land that had experienced so much pain.[3]

After an outdoor celebration at a local stadium, Tutu attended a reception in his honor at Cape Town's city hall. In order to enter the building, Tutu had to cross a group of white protesters who held signs with slogans such as "Tutu preaches sanctions, not the Gospel." But the demonstrators could not spoil the archbishop's evening. At one point Tutu climbed onto the stage where a Soweto musical group was performing and danced joyously to the music.

Desmond and Leah moved into the official residence of the archbishop in Bishopscourt, a wealthy white suburb of Cape Town. The residence was a large, attractive house with white stucco walls, designed in the distinct Cape-Dutch style. The Tutus' move to Bishopscourt violated the Group Areas Act, which required that South Africa's residential areas be segre-

gated by race, but neither Tutu nor the church was prosecuted for the vi-
olation. Tutu regularly invited black children from the townships to visit
his residence to swim in the pool and picnic on the grounds. He also
hosted multiracial Christmas parties for children at his residence.

The official name of the church Tutu now headed was the Church of
the Province of Southern Africa. It included Anglicans in South Africa,
Angola, Botswana, Lesotho, Mozambique, Namibia, Swaziland, and the
islands of St. Helena and Ascension. The church had two million members, approximately 80 percent of whom were black. Tutu quickly developed a strong bond with his bishops, both black and white. He got to
know them personally and frequently sent them letters, thank you notes,
and birthday and anniversary cards. He tried to meet with his bishops regularly for heart-to-heart talks. The bishops in turn supported their archbishop when the government criticized him. Just as the archbishop of
Canterbury had during the Eloff hearings earlier in the decade, South
Africa's Anglican bishops made it clear that an attack against Tutu would
be an attack against them. The bishops agreed as a group that world pressure was needed to end apartheid, although not all of them believed that
foreign companies should withdraw completely from South Africa.[4]

As archbishop, Tutu became busier than he had ever been before. But
he still needed time alone away from the spotlight. He continued his
habit of praying and meditating in solitude. He no longer jogged as much
as he used to, but he did take regular walks around his new neighborhood
in Bishopscourt. He relaxed by listening to classical music and reading
books on religion and politics. Leah helped keep her husband going. She
was as deeply committed to freedom as Desmond and accompanied him
on many of his trips overseas. She also made sure he didn't get too carried
away with his fame. Tutu recalled one visit he and his wife made to West
Point, the famous military academy in New York. "At the end of the visit
the cadets gave me one of their caps as a present," Tutu remembered. "It
did not fit me. Someone else would have said the cap was too small, but
my wife said, 'Your head is too big.'"[5]

Tutu received some welcome news from the United States within a
month of becoming archbishop. On October 2, 1986, the U.S. Senate
overrode President Reagan's veto and ensured the passage of a new sanctions bill. The Comprehensive Anti-Apartheid Act banned new American investments and bank loans to South Africa; prohibited imports of
South African iron, coal, and steel; ended South African landing rights at
American airports; and banned exports of oil and armaments to South
Africa. The override was a stunning defeat for the Reagan administration.
The president had wanted to give his package of milder sanctions more

time, but the Republican-controlled Senate believed that tougher measures were warranted. As prominent African American lawyer Vernon Jordan put it, many factors helped sway American public opinion in favor of sanctions, but no single individual played a greater role than Desmond Tutu.[6]

The passage of the Comprehensive Anti-Apartheid Act pleased Tutu, but he continued to press for even stronger measures. In a visit to the United States in mid-December 1986, he suggested that Americans should give the South African government a choice between greatly increased sanctions if apartheid continued or greatly increased support if apartheid was dismantled. More punitive measures could include U.S. support for UN sanctions, severing telecommunication links to South Africa, and a travel ban. Tutu still believed the leaders of Britain, West Germany, and the United States could do more to help end apartheid.

By the late 1980s, a stalemate had developed in South Africa. The government was still in control, but it had been unable to destroy the resistance movement. Authorities continued to condemn the outlawed ANC for its armed struggle and its links to communism and ruled out entering into formal negotiations with it or any other banned liberation groups. Some critics of the government believed that the ANC was worth talking to. From 1985 on, a dialogue outside of South Africa began between the ANC and white businessmen, academics, and intellectuals. Even members of P. W. Botha's own government, while condemning such meetings in public, secretly began conferring with Nelson Mandela, who had been in prison since 1962. Tutu believed more dialogue was needed with the ANC. In March 1987, he met with ANC representatives in Lusaka, Zambia, the organization's headquarters. He and the ANC delegation, which included ANC President Oliver Tambo, discussed the latest political developments in South Africa. Tutu suggested that the ANC suspend its armed struggle to encourage the South Africa government to enter into negotiations. ANC leaders considered Tutu's proposal but were not yet ready to endorse it.

One of the developments in South Africa that most disturbed Tutu was the government's widespread detention of children. Since the imposition of the nationwide state of emergency in June 1986, an estimated 30,000 people had been detained without charge, 8,000 of whom were under 18. Groups such as the Detainees Parents' Support Committee, the Black Sash, and the UDF raised an outcry over such statistics. Then, in April 1987, the government announced new curbs on protest. No statement, demonstration, or report could be made on behalf of detainees, and no article of clothing could have words or images that related to detainees. The government even banned expressions of solidarity with detainees. Violators of the new order could face up to 10 years in prison. Tutu and others in the antiapartheid movement vowed to defy the order. At a graduation ceremony at the University of the Western Cape, Tutu said, "If Christ returned to South Africa today, he would almost certainly be detained under the present security laws, because of his concern for the poor, the hungry, and the oppressed."[7] Tutu later held a special service at St. George's Cathedral, during which he promised to urge his congregations to launch a peaceful campaign on behalf of detainees. Three days later, he and 46 other Anglican clergymen wrote to State President Botha, saying they would continue to speak out on behalf of detainees, even if it was against the law. The South African police commissioner announced shortly thereafter that the government's latest restrictions did not apply to statements made at bona fide religious services. It was a small concession, but an important one.

Tutu's high visibility and international stature continued to shield him from government retaliation, at least in public. One journalist perceptively remarked that "Tutu seemed to possess an almost diplomatic immunity to speak his mind."[8] But that didn't mean that the government restrained itself completely. At one point during Tutu's tenure as archbishop, government agents secretly nailed a baboon fetus to a tree in his yard at Bishopscourt as a form of intimidation. Other anonymous detractors painted images of the hammer and sickle (symbols of communism) on the walls of his residence. Because the government usually refrained from taking official action against Tutu, white frustration and anger often took the form of harassment.

Tutu obviously continued to elicit strong reactions from South Africans. One 1987 poll indicated that 35 percent of white Anglicans were dissatisfied with their church; two-thirds of the malcontents traced their anger to Archbishop Tutu and the South African Council of Churches. But in a poll conducted by the *Sowetan* newspaper that same year, the paper's mostly black readers listed Tutu as the third-most desirable leader of South Africa, just behind Nelson Mandela and Oliver Tambo. Tutu hoped Mandela and his colleagues would be released from prison and allowed to return from exile so he could concentrate on being archbishop. Despite his high political profile, Tutu insisted that he was not interested in political office.

The public's perception of P. W. Botha also varied. All but a few blacks opposed his government, but many whites—Afrikaners and English speakers—endorsed his leadership and embraced the reforms he introduced. Others accused him of jeopardizing their future. This white back-

lash grew from the mid-1980s on. The far-right Conservative Party opposed his abolition of the pass laws in 1986, lamented the end of the
whites-only parliament, and favored re-imposing the bans on interracial
sex and marriage. The Conservative Party gained seats in the May 1987
election and became the official opposition in the House of Assembly.
This increased threat from the right slowed down Botha's reforms and encouraged him to crack down even harder on the antiapartheid movement.

Tutu continued his appeals for international support after the May
1987 election. During a trip to Brazil, he called for all nations to break
diplomatic relations with South Africa. He then traveled to the United
States, where he was awarded the Pacem in Terris Peace and Freedom
Award in Davenport, Iowa, in recognition of his efforts to end apartheid
peacefully. At a press conference before the awards ceremony, Tutu said
that although he had given up calling for Western leaders to toughen
their stance against apartheid, he still believed in appealing directly to the
people.[9]

Tutu sparked fresh controversy during a June 1987 visit to Mozambique, where he visited churches and met with President Joachim
Chissano. At a news conference in Maputo, Tutu was asked if he thought
the time had come for black South Africans to use violence in the fight
for freedom. He replied that he would tell the world when he thought that
day had come, but it hadn't yet. Filtering Tutu's remarks for local con-
sumption, some South African journalists reported that the archbishop
"planned to announce the day black South Africans could turn to violence."[10] The firestorm of controversy that erupted threatened to engulf
Tutu upon his return home. In fact, the outcry among white South
Africans was so great that Tutu told his personal assistant where he kept
his will, in case he was assassinated when he returned to South Africa.
When Tutu arrived back in the country, his staff rented a car to take him
to Johannesburg. Just before Tutu and his aides drove off, an onlooker noticed something strange on one of the vehicle's front tires. The tread was
completely gone and wires were sticking out instead. Luckily the damage
was noticed in time, and aides rented a new vehicle. Someone had apparently tried to sabotage Tutu's car, although who might have done so remains a mystery.[11]

As absorbed as Tutu was in trying to end apartheid, he realized that
conflicts between different black groups threatened to prolong white rule.
In November 1987, he sought to stop deadly clashes between UDF and
Inkatha supporters in Natal. At a service in Pietermaritzburg, he told listeners that black South Africans were delaying their liberation by fighting each other. He and other church leaders later met with UDF and

Inkatha representatives in Durban in an effort to promote peace, but the violence continued.

Nineteen eighty-eight was probably the most difficult year yet for the antiapartheid movement. On February 24, the government banned the UDF, 16 other groups, and 18 prominent antiapartheid activists. Religious leaders such as Tutu believed that the churches needed to fill the gap, even if it aggravated the already-tense relationship between church and state. On February 29, Tutu and more than 20 other church leaders led a procession from St. George's Cathedral to the parliament building next door. Dressed in clerical robes and holding Bibles, the leaders sought to submit a petition to the government protesting the recent ban on the UDF and other antiapartheid groups. The police had other ideas. They ordered the group to disperse, but instead Tutu and his fellow clerics knelt down and linked arms. The police then arrested Tutu and his colleagues and sprayed the remaining demonstrators with water cannons. The clergymen were released a few hours later.

Vowing to continue the work of the banned organizations no matter what the consequences, Tutu and his allies launched the Committee for the Defense of Democracy. Minister of Law and Order Adrian Vlok then warned the church leaders against embarking on political activities or protests. Tutu and Allan Boesak held a joint service at St. George's Cathedral on March 13, 1988, despite Vlok's warning. They said the church was the only institution black South Africans had left to protest apartheid nonviolently. On the day of the service, police set up roadblocks and prepared to use water cannons and tear gas against participants. Police videotaped those entering the church and monitored the service from the inside. Their presence did not deter Tutu from pledging to intensify his opposition to repression. In his remarks, Tutu commented on the government's new strategy of labeling church leaders "revolutionary." "If it is revolution to say I work for a South Africa that is nonracial, if it is revolution to say I am working for a South Africa that is truly democratic, if it is revolution to say I am working for a South Africa where black and white and yellow and green can walk together arm in arm, then, my friends, I am for that."[12]

Tutu had one of his rare meetings with P. W. Botha on March 16, 1988, in Cape Town. The conversation began cordially, but then Botha angrily accused Tutu of encouraging people to break the law, as he had during the February 29 procession near Parliament. Tutu began to understand why the state president had been given the nickname "Big Crocodile." But Tutu was in no mood to be snapped at. "One thing you've got to know is that I'm not a small boy," he told Botha. "You're not my headmaster."

Tutu said his love for South Africa was probably greater than Botha's because black South Africans fought against the Nazis, while Botha's people didn't. This only fueled the president's anger. Tutu later admitted that they both lost their temper and bickered "like little boys." But Tutu could not hold his tongue. "I don't know whether that is how Jesus would have handled it," he recalled. "But at that moment, I actually didn't mind how Jesus would have handled it. I was going to handle it my way."[13]

The confrontation between the two men was far from over. During their meeting on March 16, Botha handed Tutu a letter addressed to him, accusing the churches of being pawns of the ANC and the South African Communist Party. Botha's letter also accused the ANC of seeking to create an "atheistic Marxist state" in South Africa. From Botha's vantage point, the churches were furthering the cause of Marxism and atheism by their actions. He released the letter to the press and members of Parliament without consulting Tutu. This was part of a long-standing effort to discredit Tutu by linking him to communism and violence. Despite the state president's charges, archbishop of Canterbury Runcie wrote a letter in support of Tutu after the letter was released. Forty-four prominent South African theologians did the same in a letter to the *Argus* newspaper. They labeled the government's attacks on Tutu and other church leaders as unjustified and unchristian.

Tutu replied to Botha with a letter of his own in early April. His letter was one of the most powerful, sweeping statements he had ever written on the role of the church in South Africa. In it, Tutu insisted that his opposition to apartheid was based on biblical principles, not Marxism or the ANC. He wrote, "Apartheid has said that ultimately people are intended for separation. You have carried out policies enshrined in the Population Registration Act, the Group Areas Act, segregated education, health, etc. The Bible teaches quite unequivocally that people are created for fellowship, for togetherness, not for alienation, apartness, enmity, and division. (Gen 2:18; Gen 11:1–9; 1 Cor 12:12–13; Rom 12:3–5; Gal 3:28; Acts 17:26)." The rest of the letter contained multiple references to the Bible to show that Christianity and apartheid were incompatible. Tutu even quoted an Afrikaans theologian from the Dutch Reformed Church who wrote in 1947 that it was the church's duty to work for social justice. Tutu wrote about his own efforts urging a peaceful end to apartheid but noted that his many warnings had been ignored. "How much time has been wasted and how many lives have been lost trying to beautify apartheid through cosmetic improvements when the pillars of a vicious system still remain firmly in place," he wrote. If the state president undertook several key steps, then Tutu would publicly urge South Africans to give him a chance. These steps would be to lift the state of emergency, unban political organizations, release detainees and political prisoners, permit exiles to return, and begin negotiations for a new government. Assuring Botha of his good faith, Tutu concluded, "We long for the day when black and white will live amicably and harmoniously together in the new South Africa."[14]

Despite all of his negative experiences at the hands of whites—Vorster, P. W. Botha, the police, the white-owned press, the threats—Tutu had not become antiwhite. This was due in large part to his own personal history. His early role model, Trevor Huddleston, and his positive experiences with whites in Britain had done much to temper any racial bitterness. He also admired the courageous white South African church leaders who were his contemporaries, such as Beyers Naudé, Peter Storey, and others. Groups such as the Black Sash and the End Conscription Campaign showed that there were whites in South Africa who wanted real change. These and other examples had long convinced Tutu that the enemy was apartheid, not white people.

P. W. Botha was not as magnanimous. He was so angered by the church leaders' defiance—and his perception that they supported communism, terrorism, and revolution—that he secretly ordered government agents to blow up Khotso House, the SACC headquarters in Johannesburg. The deed was done in the predawn hours of August 31, 1988. Although the building was badly damaged by the blast, no one was killed (21 people were injured). No one confessed to the bombing afterward, but the police suggested that it might have been caused by explosives that the SACC allegedly stored in the building. The notion that the SACC kept explosives was preposterous; it was merely another attempt to link antiapartheid church leaders to violence.

Because his mission to generate worldwide opposition to apartheid had largely succeeded by the late 1980s, Tutu felt freer to speak his mind on other issues. In February 1989, he spoke about tensions between blacks and Jews in South Africa and the United States after receiving an award at the Stephen Wise Free Synagogue in New York City. He said he saw some parallels between the treatment of black South Africans under apartheid and the treatment of Palestinians under Israeli rule. But, he said, "We thank God that Israel as a nation has come into being. It has a right to territorial integrity and fundamental security."[15] He also condemned all forms of terrorism. He urged American Jews to pressure Israel to end its military cooperation with the South African government and to reach a settlement with the Palestinians. He even suggested that he and Elie Wiesel (the 1986 Nobel Peace Prize winner, author, and holocaust survivor) help mediate the Israeli-Palestinian conflict. Ten months after this speech, Tutu visited Israel as a guest of the Anglican bishop of Jerusalem. The chief rabbis in Jerusalem refused to see Tutu because he had expressed sympathy toward the Palestinians. Tutu's perspectives on the Israeli-Palestinian conflict would continue to generate strong feelings in the years to come.

Tutu also spoke out about human rights in the wider world. In September 1987, he had been elected president of the All-Africa Conference of Churches, reflecting the esteem with which he was viewed by the rest of Africa. He visited Zaire in his capacity as president in February 1989. During a speech in Kinshasa, he deplored the human rights violations and lack of freedom in Africa. He lamented the fact that African leaders oppressed their own people. Zaire was home to one of Africa's longest-ruling dictators, Mobutu Sese Seko, but this did not deter Tutu from speaking his mind. God sides with the oppressed, he reminded his audience, not just in South Africa, but everywhere. He conveyed a similar message during visits to Panama and Nicaragua in March 1989.

South Africa's political landscape shifted significantly in 1989. P. W. Botha suffered a stroke in January, which weakened, but did not incapacitate him. Once he recovered, he decided to continue on as state president but give up the leadership of the National Party. F. W. de Klerk took his place as the new National Party leader. This transition would gradually erode Botha's power and influence in the months ahead. A month after Botha's stroke, Tutu and other church leaders met with Minister of Law and Order Vlok for two and a half hours and urged him to release detainees. Vlok agreed to release almost 300 detainees who had recently staged a hunger strike, although 1,000 others would remain in detention. Tutu was pleased by Vlok's decision, despite its limited scope. "It does give our people hope," he said. "It shows that success can also be achieved through negotiation, through nonviolent action."[16] Five months later in Oslo, Tutu said the world should help pressure the South African government to go to the negotiating table. He stressed that the goal was not to defeat or destroy the government, but to force it to negotiate.

The escalating pressures facing South Africa gave Tutu confidence that the government could in fact be forced to negotiate. Between early 1986 and mid-1988, 114 American companies withdrew from South Africa. Sanctions had intensified from the United States, the European Community, and the British Commonwealth. The South African economy began a downward spiral. Despite the state of emergency, the security forces had been unable to extinguish internal unrest completely. Botha's inability to solve South Africa's deepening crisis cost him the support of his cabinet as 1989 progressed. Following an angry confrontation with his colleagues, Botha suddenly resigned on August 14, 1989. F. W. de Klerk, the Transvaal-based National Party leader, became the new state president. His political stance was ambiguous. He expressed his opposition to the old version of "grand" apartheid, but he still supported some forms of residential, educational, and political segregation. Whether he would introduce significant changes to South Africa was unclear. When de Klerk became state president in August, Tutu was initially unimpressed. He didn't see that anything had changed, except that the president's initials had changed from P. W. to F. W.

Opposition groups saw an opening. The banned UDF, now reformulated as the Mass Democratic Movement, planned a major defiance campaign during the run up to elections in September. Protests escalated that August. Black workers went on strike nationwide to protest a new law limiting strikes. Antiapartheid groups called for a national protest over the upcoming segregated parliamentary elections. Tutu endorsed the growing mood of defiance sweeping the country and actively contributed to it. In one incident, Tutu tried to mediate between police and black students before violence could erupt at a protest march. Tutu urged the police to refrain from using force on the marchers, but as he and the students left a church, the police fired tear gas at them. Tutu was not injured, but he was forced to breathe the acrid smoke that had become all too familiar to township activists. On August 19, 1989, Tutu participated in a day of protests at some of Cape Town's whites-only beaches. He and his fellow demonstrators decided to enter a whites-only beach at Strand, on Cape Town's False Bay. To get to the beach, they had to cross police roadblocks and face officers with dogs, whips, and tear gas. The policeman in charge said that if the protesters did not disperse, he would order his officers to fire live ammunition into the crowd. Tutu did manage to walk on the beach briefly, but once he left, police set their dogs on those who remained and fired rubber bullets into the unarmed crowd.

Despite such police callousness, the defiance continued. On September 1, Tutu, Leah, and 34 others protested police brutality during a march outside St. George's Cathedral. They were arrested and released shortly thereafter. The next day, the South African police sprayed protesters with purple dye as they held demonstrations on the streets of central Cape Town. Tutu gave a pep talk to demonstrators who sought refuge from the police at St. George's Cathedral. He told them, "The prize for which we are striving is freedom, is freedom for all of us, freedom for those people standing outside [the police], freedom for them! Because, you see, when we are free...they will be here...joining with us celebrating that freedom, and not standing outside there stopping us from becoming free."[17]

Election day, September 6, 1989, was unusually bloody. More than 20 people were killed by police during a series of protests in Cape Town's black townships. Two million workers stayed home to protest the election. Horrified by the day's violence, Tutu and Allan Boesak called for a mass protest march on September 13 in honor of those killed. Such a march would clearly violate the state of emergency regulations, but Tutu and Boesak were resolute. They urged diplomats from key western nations to monitor the march, and they received the support of the white mayor of Cape Town, who agreed to participate. De Klerk, newly installed as president, decided to let the march go ahead. On September 13, 1989, 30,000 people marched for peace in the streets of central Cape Town. It was one of the largest demonstrations in South African history. Tutu was exhilarated that the march was so successful and peaceful. Speaking to thousands of participants from the balcony of Cape Town's city hall, Tutu said that the struggle for freedom was unstoppable. After the march in Cape Town, other marches were held in Johannesburg, East London, Durban, and Bloemfontein. Tutu believed that such demonstrations would convince de Klerk that sweeping changes were inevitable.

On October 10, 1989, de Klerk announced the impending release of eight key anti-apartheid leaders, including Mandela's longtime colleagues Walter Sisulu and Ahmed Kathrada, who had been imprisoned since 1963. The next day, Tutu, Boesak, and SACC General Secretary Frank Chikane traveled to Pretoria and met with de Klerk for almost three hours. The church leaders said that they would recommend that sanctions be suspended if de Klerk took steps to normalize political activity, such as ending the emergency, unbanning political organizations, and releasing key leaders. The talks were considerably more constructive than those Tutu had had with P. W. Botha. But Tutu was still cautious. No concrete agreements had been reached, but the talks lasted almost three times longer than originally scheduled, which seemed to indicate de Klerk's seriousness. Tutu had no idea just how serious de Klerk was.

NOTES

1. Shirley du Boulay, *Tutu: Voice of the Voiceless* (Grand Rapids, MI: William B. Eerdmans, 1988), pp. 250–51.

2. Kerry Kennedy Cuomo, *Speak Truth to Power: Human Rights Defenders Who Are Changing Our World* (New York: Crown, 2000), p. 60.

3. Desmond Tutu, *The Rainbow People of God: The Making of a Peaceful Revolution*, ed. John Allen (New York: Doubleday, 1994), pp. 113–27.

4. Michael Nuttall, *Number Two to Tutu: A Memoir* (Pietermaritzburg: Cluster Publications, 2003), pp. 21–24.

5. Desmond Tutu, *The Essential Desmond Tutu*, comp. John Allen (Cape Town: David Philip, 1997), p. 78.

6. Du Boulay, *Tutu*, p. 197.

7. Du Boulay, *Tutu*, pp. 262–63.

8. Steven Mufson, *Fighting Years: Black Resistance and the Struggle for a New South Africa* (Boston: Beacon Press, 1990), p. 324.

9. "Tutu Rakes U.S. Policy on S. Africa," *Quad City Times* (Davenport, IA), 26 May 1987.

10. Tutu, *The Rainbow People of God*, p. 130.

11. Tutu, *The Rainbow People of God*, pp. 129–32.

12. Tutu, *The Rainbow People of God*, p. 142.

13. Tutu, *The Essential Desmond Tutu*, pp. 47–48.

14. Desmond Tutu, letter to P. W. Botha, 8 April 1988, *Ecunews* 14 (April 1988): pp. 14–16.

15. "Tutu Asks US Jews to Urge Palestinian Pact," *New York Times*, 4 February 1989.

16. "Pretoria Said to Plan Release of 300 Detainees," *New York Times*, 17 February 1989.

17. Tutu, *The Rainbow People of God*, p. 181.

Chapter 13

WITNESSING THE BIRTH OF A
NEW SOUTH AFRICA

On February 2, 1990, South Africa once again made news all over the world. In his opening speech to the South African Parliament that day, State President F. W. de Klerk made a series of historic announcements. He unbanned the ANC, PAC, and the South African Communist Party; promised to release most political prisoners, including Nelson Mandela; and pledged to begin negotiations for a new South Africa free from apartheid. His speech took almost everyone by surprise. Following the televised address, spontaneous celebrations broke out in South Africa's major cities. In Johannesburg, people danced in the streets and sang with joy, while passersby honked their horns and waved. Tutu was overjoyed when he heard the speech. It had, he said, "certainly taken my breath away."[1] He quickly telephoned de Klerk to congratulate him. When asked about the speech later that day, Tutu said, "I found it exhilarating, quite astounding that we seem to be at the dawn of the new South Africa for which so many people have striven."[2]

Many factors contributed to de Klerk's breathtaking initiatives. The end of the cold war lessened the government's fears of a communist takeover. International pressure had begun to undermine the economy. The liberation struggle had been beaten back, but not broken. And Mandela's statesmanship during years of secret talks impressed the government and helped create a climate for dialogue. De Klerk believed that apartheid had become unworkable and that the time had come for bold reforms. P. W. Botha was no longer in office to stand in his way.

Eight days after his historic speech, de Klerk announced that Mandela would be released on February 11, 1990, after 27 1/2 years in prison. Tutu was so overjoyed at the news that he danced with glee as photographers snapped pictures. He felt sure that negotiations for a new government were just around the corner. Commenting on Mandela's impending release, Tutu said, "It is saying to us, God hears...God acts, God is really involved. We've been praying so long and it seemed like our prayers were just going into a void. Now [what we prayed for] is happening.... We are all going to be free together, black and white."[3] Once negotiations began, Tutu promised to travel the world asking for countries to reinvest.

On February 11, 71-year-old Nelson Mandela walked through the gates of Victor Verster prison outside of Cape Town hand-in-hand with his wife Winnie, as crowds of journalists, photographers, and well-wishers watched. Later that day, Mandela addressed thousands of people from the balcony of Cape Town's city hall. He spent his first night of freedom at Tutu's residence in Bishopscourt. He had long admired the role the churches played in resisting apartheid and viewed Tutu as "the archbishop of the people."[4] Tutu in turn greatly admired Mandela's eloquence, courage, strength, and dignity. The morning after his release, Mandela held his first press conference in Tutu's backyard. Like the archbishop, he would impress observers with his lack of bitterness, his stress on reconciliation, and his unconquerable desire for freedom.

Tutu led a service of thanksgiving at St. George's Cathedral on March 6, 1990. He admitted that many might have begun to doubt God's power because God didn't seem inclined to intervene after years of oppression and struggle. "Even now you keep pinching yourself to see what has happened," Tutu said. He noted that former enemies were finally beginning to see each other as brothers. He also expressed his gratitude to overseas friends who supported the struggle, to de Klerk for his courageous actions, and to South Africans for their determination to be free. "And so friends," he told the congregation, "we have come to give thanks for the beginning of the end of apartheid, the dawn of a new South Africa. We come to give thanks to God for the possibilities about which we have been dreaming that we seem to be realizing."[5] Tutu was clearly jubilant that the crisis in his country seemed to be ending. The long struggle for justice had been worthwhile. As it turned out, Tutu had no idea how difficult the next few years would be.

Because political leaders had been unbanned and released, Tutu hoped to adopt a lower political profile in the 1990s. He wanted more time to minister directly to people in need in poor townships and squatter camps. He also expected to have more time for quiet meditation. He didn't intend to ignore political developments completely, however. He reserved the right to say if a particular policy was inconsistent with Christianity, but he would not overtly endorse a particular party or platform. In August 1990, Tutu and the Anglican synod of bishops agreed to prohibit Anglican clergy from joining political parties. The church leaders worried that partisan clergy might not be accepted by those with opposing political agendas. Tutu was especially concerned about the long-standing tensions between the ANC and Inkatha. Since the clergy might be called upon to mediate in the conflict, Tutu believed they should not side with any one particular group.

Turf wars between the ANC and Inkatha erupted in 1990, especially in the province of Natal. Then, as both groups competed for black support, clashes spread to the Transvaal. By September 1990, almost 1,000 people had been killed in such clashes. As the violence escalated, Tutu's initial plan to withdraw from politics faded. He began to embark on shuttle diplomacy among officials from the government, the homelands, and the liberation movement in an effort to promote peace. He participated in several mediation efforts in black townships on the Witwatersrand, the area near Johannesburg. He joined church delegations that met with families who lost loved ones or lost their homes in the violence. In August 1990, Tutu and SACC leader Frank Chikane embarked on a peace mission to Kagiso, a township on the West Rand. An angry crowd greeted them by shouting, "No more peace, we want arms!"[6] But Tutu was not one to buckle under pressure. He said the recent fighting gave the impression that black South Africans weren't ready to govern themselves. He urged the residents to forsake violence so that a new South Africa could be born.

To his utter horror, Tutu found himself once again presiding over mass funerals. At a funeral in Soweto on August 27, 1990, Tutu denied rumors that the violence was tribal. He acknowledged concerns that the police were encouraging different black factions to attack one another. Addressing the mourners, Tutu asked, "My dear brothers and sisters, my dear children, why is it that we blacks can be bribed to kill one another? What is wrong with us? Don't we have a pride? Are we ashamed of being black?" Then Tutu urged the crowd to repeat after him, "I am proud I am black. We will strive for freedom. We are not going to fight each other. We want peace! We want harmony! We want togetherness!"[7]

Unfortunately, violence only seemed to get worse. Between September 3 and 5, 1990, approximately 36 people were killed in Sebokeng, a township south of Johannesburg. Tutu was attending an Anglican synod of bishops in Lesotho at the time. When he heard the news, he retreated to his room and broke down in tears. Then he suspended the synod and urged his bishops to travel with him to Sebokeng. Upon arrival, Tutu visited the wounded and preached at a church in the township. He learned that much of the violence had emanated from workers' hostels, whose members were often Zulu rural dwellers loyal to Inkatha. Tutu urged residents not to seek revenge and not to allow others to divide them. Hatred and revenge were like acid, he said, because they corroded the human spirit.

After hearing that whites had been among the attackers in Sebokeng, Tutu quickly arranged a meeting with F. W. de Klerk. He and an Anglican Church delegation met de Klerk in Pretoria on September 10, 1990, to discuss the recent violence. The church leaders feared that a "third force" was encouraging violence in order to prolong apartheid and derail the negotiation process. Tutu suspected that right-wing elements existed in de Klerk's own security forces that might be fomenting violence. Unless de Klerk took action against those elements, Tutu said, "we are for the birds."[8] De Klerk promised to investigate. Two months later, Tutu convened a summit of black political leaders at his home in Bishopscourt. He invited leaders of the homelands and liberation groups but was unable to persuade Inkatha leader Mangosuthu Buthelezi to attend. Despite the summit, violence continued. South Africa seemed to be on a roller-coaster ride. At the pinnacle of euphoria earlier in the year, the nation was now plummeting to the depths of despair over violence.

Tutu didn't blame just the de Klerk government for violence. In a sermon he gave at St. George's Cathedral in late March 1991, Tutu traced the violence to the legacy of apartheid, poverty, and the culture of intolerance in South Africa. He also said that black communities had become too desensitized toward violence. "It seems to me that we in the black community have lost our sense of ubuntu—our humaneness, caring, hospitality, our sense of connectedness, our sense that my humanity is bound up with your humanity," he lamented.[9] He urged black South Africans to develop a tradition of agreeing to disagree and to ensure that members of political organizations became more disciplined.

The news was not all bleak. De Klerk's government repealed the main apartheid legislation in the early 1990s, including the Population Registration Act, the Land Act, and the Group Areas Act. Tutu was part of a group of church and business leaders that brokered a peace accord between the government and South Africa's main political parties in 1991. Tutu spent the latter part of 1991 on sabbatical at the Candler School of Theology at Emory University in Atlanta. Toward the end of his sabbatical, the first Convention for a Democratic South Africa (CODESA) was held, bringing together the government, homeland leaders, and the liberation movements under one roof to discuss South Africa's future.

Unfortunately, 1992 was the worst year yet for South African political violence. Tutu became convinced that a rogue element in the security forces was trying to subvert the negotiation process. As he wrote in the *Los Angeles Times,* "Until 1990, our police force was extremely efficient. It could ferret out insurgents secretly infiltrated into the country. Now people are openly carrying weapons, killing others in broad daylight. And we are supposed to believe that the police have suddenly become inept."[10] Tutu urged de Klerk to end the violence, just as he would if whites were victims.

The single-worst outbreak of violence occurred on the night of June 17, 1992. Several hundred armed men attacked the black community of Boipatong, south of Johannesburg, killing 46 residents, including young children. The attackers were mostly Zulu migrant workers from a nearby hostel. After the killings, Boipatong residents accused the police of aiding the attackers. De Klerk planned a visit to Boipatong to convey his sympathy, but angry residents forced his motorcade to flee the area. In the ensuing demonstrations, police killed eight more Boipatong residents. Tutu and a pair of Anglican bishops rushed to the community on June 19 to console families of the victims. Clearly in anguish over the violence, Tutu sensed that South Africa was "on the brink of a disaster." His goodwill toward de Klerk's government had evaporated. "We thought they had changed...I don't think they have changed," he said. "They were looking for a way of getting the world to reduce its pressure on them." Tutu insisted that the perpetrators of the Boipatong attack be brought to justice. In a sermon he preached in Cape Town following the massacre, he called for an international monitoring force to patrol South Africa's crisis-ridden townships. If such a force was not deployed quickly, he warned, the country might descend into a "Yugoslavian nightmare." He said that unless the government did more to reduce violence, South Africa's invitation to the 1992 Olympics in Barcelona should be withdrawn. (South Africa had been banned from the Olympics since 1964.) The struggle to put international pressure on South Africa was beginning again, much to the archbishop's dismay. Finally, Tutu urged white South Africans to take a stand against the recent violence: "We are going to be free. We want you to be with us when we are free. We want you to share with us, we want you to be human with us, we want you to walk tall with us. Will you? Will you stand up?" Tutu clearly feared that if the violence wasn't brought under control, South Africa might be destroyed by civil war.[11]

Nelson Mandela agreed. As leader of the ANC, he said he could not negotiate with a government that allowed violence to escalate. He accused de Klerk's government of "murdering our people."[12] Shortly after the Boipatong massacre, the ANC suspended its participation in negotiations. Tutu later met with de Klerk, who assured him that the government would do more to end violence. Placing his trust in de Klerk once again, Tutu then dropped his call for the Olympic ban. Eventually it was revealed that the South African government had secretly funded Inkatha in the 1990s so that it could serve as a counterweight to the ANC. Some elements of the security forces had indeed been provoking violence in an attempt to postpone the end of white minority rule.

Negotiations between the ANC and the government only resumed following a crisis in Bisho, the capital of the Ciskei homeland, in September 1992. Homeland police there fired on thousands of pro-ANC demonstrators, killing 29 and injuring dozens more. After the carnage, the ANC and the South African government realized that they had to negotiate before violence consumed them all. But just as the government and the ANC resumed talks, Buthelezi pulled Inkatha out of negotiations. He accused the two sides of trying to marginalize him, his party, and the Zulu people. Meanwhile, violence between Inkatha and the ANC continued. In the Natal province alone, at least 2,000 people were killed in clashes between the two organizations from 1990 to 1992. Each side blamed the other for the violence. Then one violent act threatened to jeopardize the entire transition out of apartheid.

On April 10, 1993, a white immigrant from Poland assassinated Chris Hani, a highly popular leader in the ANC and the South African Communist Party. Hani was one of the most admired black leaders in South Africa, especially by young militants from the townships. After news of the killing spread, black anger and grief threatened to explode into more violence. Mandela appeared on South African television to appeal for calm. Although Tutu was not a communist—he believed communism ignored the need for God in people's lives—he greatly admired Chris Hani. He spoke at Hani's funeral in Soweto on April 19. Before 100,000 bereaved souls, Tutu paid tribute to Hani's commitment to peace and insisted that Hani's death would not interrupt South Africa's march to victory. A more divisive leader could have used the occasion to rail against whites and preach revenge. Instead, Tutu preached reconciliation. He sought to boost the confidence of his listeners and ensure that they rededicated themselves to freedom for all, black and white. Reminded of the prospect of approaching liberation—which no assassin's bullets could stop—the crowd's grief transformed into exuberance.

Two months later, Tutu worked behind the scenes to arrange a meeting between Mandela and Buthelezi. The opportunity arose while Tutu was in Pietermaritzburg to consecrate a new bishop and witness the unveiling of a statue of Mohandas Gandhi. Hearing that both leaders were in town to attend different events, Tutu convinced both men to agree to a future meeting. Buthelezi and Mandela met in Kempton Park in June 1993 and appeared at a press conference with Archbishop Tutu afterward. The talks, which lasted 10 hours, strengthened the bonds of mutual respect between both men, whose parties were still engaged in deadly clashes. Buthelezi refused to endorse the proposed April 1994 election date (open to all races), but he did agree to join Mandela in appealing for peace.

Until 1993, virtually all victims of South African political violence had been black. But that year, some radical black groups, frustrated by the slow pace of negotiations and embittered by years of mistreatment, began to launch attacks against whites. On July 25, 1993, several heavily armed black men burst into a suburban Cape Town church during a Sunday evening service, lobbed hand grenades at the congregation and opened fire with machine guns. The attack killed 11 worshippers and wounded more than 50. Most of the victims were white. Tutu was horrified by the attack. Four days later, he participated in a rally for peace at the Cape Town city hall attended by Capetonians of all races and faiths. As he had at Chris Hani's funeral, Tutu urged his listeners not to let perpetrators of evil derail the march toward freedom. As for the evildoers, Tutu said, "They have reached the bottom of depravity in attacking and so desecrating a place of divine worship and adoration, God's sanctuary." A leader less committed to reconciliation might have ignored or downplayed white deaths, but not Tutu. He stressed that "one death is one death too many."[13] Some antiwhite violence continued. A month after the church attack, American Fulbright scholar Amy Biehl was killed by a group of black militants in Guguletu (one of Cape Town's black townships) as she was giving some black friends a ride home. But despite some highly publicized white deaths, most of the victims of South Africa's violence were black. The mounting death toll—some 18,000 between 1984 and 1993—finally convinced most South Africans that only one thing could stop the killing—a political settlement.

After years of turmoil and uncertainty, negotiators from the government and the ANC finally agreed to an interim constitution in November 1993. Control over the government passed to the multiparty Transitional Executive Council, and a nationwide election was scheduled for April 1994. After the election, a Government of National Unity would take office for five years, ensuring that all major parties were represented in Parliament and the cabinet. Inkatha and the white right refused to endorse the plan, believing that they had been sidelined during the negotiation process. Buthelezi announced that Inkatha would boycott the election. Tutu urged Buthelezi to cooperate, but the Inkatha leader was not ready to budge.

Then, a week before the April 1994 election, Buthelezi agreed to participate after intensive international mediation. As the election approached, Tutu's picture was shown on posters urging South Africans to vote. The captions on the posters read, "Someday we will all be free—That day has come—Please vote."[14] South Africa experienced a last spasm of violence in the days before the election. Bombs exploded in Johannesburg, the East Rand, and Pretoria, killing more than 20 people. But these efforts to derail the election failed. From April 26 to April 29, people flocked to the polls in South Africa's first democratic, all-race election. Millions of South Africans had never been allowed to vote before. Some people waited all day to cast their ballots, standing patiently in lines that twisted and curved as far as the eye could see.

Tutu cast his ballot on Wednesday, April 27. Before leaving home to vote, he went to the private chapel at his Bishopscourt residence and thanked God for bringing that day to South Africa. Tutu was 62 years old, but this was the first time he had ever been allowed to vote. As Tutu entered the voting station in Guguletu, he shouted, "The day has come!" to the cheers of black onlookers. Many had been waiting to vote since 4:00 A.M. Tutu marked his ballot and slipped it into a wooden box. Then he gleefully clasped his hands over his head in triumph and said, "Friends, here we are—this is what we were all working for, it's here today, here we are voting!"[15] Tutu later called the election a "religious experience" for the nation—a "miracle." He noted how people who had been divided for so long suddenly discovered that they shared a common love for a common country. In his opinion, everyone who voted was transformed. Blacks' humanity was restored, and whites were relieved of their tremendous guilt. After voting, Tutu wrote,

> We are still on Cloud Nine and have not yet touched terra firma. Our feelings are difficult to put into words. I said it was like falling in love. That is why it seems the sun is shining brighter, the flowers seem more beautiful, the birds sing more sweetly and the people...are really more beautiful. They are smiling, they are walking taller than before April 27. They have suddenly discovered that they are all South Africans.

He hailed the peaceful election as "a victory for all South Africans, for democracy and freedom."[16]

Nelson Mandela and the ANC received nearly 63 percent of the vote; second and third place went to de Klerk's National Party with 20 percent and Buthelezi's Inkatha Freedom Party with 10.5 percent. These parties would form the new Government of National Unity. On May 9, 1994, the newly elected National Assembly met for the first time in Cape Town. Tutu's eyes filled with tears as he watched the proceedings unfold. After the assembly met, Tutu presided over a celebration from the balcony at city hall. To the massive cheers of 70,000 people, Tutu proclaimed that South Africa had been liberated at last. He then introduced South Africa's new leaders: President Nelson Mandela and Deputy Presidents Thabo Mbeki (ANC) and F. W. de Klerk.

On May 10, 1994, Mandela was inaugurated as South Africa's first black president at an outdoor ceremony at the Union Buildings in Pretoria. Dignitaries from all over the world gathered to witness the historic ceremony, from U.S. first lady Hillary Clinton to Cuban dictator Fidel Castro. As "archbishop of the people," Tutu led a prayer at the ceremony. He thanked God for enabling South Africa to overcome its long period of injustice and alienation and for enabling it to emerge from darkness into a new dawn "where all of us, black and white together, will count not because of irrelevancies such as race, gender, status, or skin color, but because of our intrinsic worth as those created in your own image."[17] Now Tutu could truly call South Africans "the rainbow people of God." The whole country was in a state of euphoria after the elections and the inauguration. Many believed that South Africa had left its painful past behind and was headed for a bright future. Apartheid, the system that had marred the lives of South Africans for so long, was history. South Africa's nightmare had ended; its dream had come true.

As the nation underwent its historic transformation, Tutu began to ponder his role in a post-apartheid South Africa. He heard God's voice during a moment of reflection at Bishopscourt. As Tutu described it, "God was saying, 'I want you to tell the people of this land that I love them, that each one is precious to me, that they are made by love, for love, to love, and that there is not enough time left over to hate, to nurse grudges.'"[18] Tutu believed it was his duty to help heal a nation wounded by the past. In a sense, one struggle was over, but another was just beginning.

It wasn't long before Tutu reasserted himself as the conscience of the nation. In August 1994, South African members of Parliament (MPs) voted to give themselves, the president, and the cabinet a substantial raise. The move triggered widespread dismay among the South African public, which had long been wary of government corruption. Tutu arranged a meeting with President Mandela to voice his reservations about the salary increases. He believed the raises sent the wrong signal to a country still suffering from widespread poverty. As he told reporters, "They [the new parliament] missed a golden opportunity in my view to demonstrate that they were serious about stopping the gravy train. They stopped the gravy train only long enough to get on it."[19] The combination of Tutu's remarks and popular pressure forced officials to rethink their plans. Before long, the president and the cabinet reduced their salaries, although the raise for MPs remained intact.

Tutu's words not only reverberated within South Africa but in the wider world as well. Since the early 1980s, he had begun publishing collections of his sermons, speeches, and statements for an international readership. His first collection was entitled *Crying in the Wilderness: The Struggle for Justice in South Africa* (1982, 1986, 1990). He followed that up with *Hope and Suffering* (1984), *The Rainbow People of God* (1994), and *An African Prayer Book* (1995). The latter publication contained prayers from all over Africa along with commentaries from Tutu.

In October 1994, Tutu announced his intention to retire as archbishop in 1996. A year before his retirement, he explained his decision at a provincial synod in Kimberley:

> It is right that a change of leadership should happen now. We have been involved very much in the *against* mode, fighting against apartheid. Our countries have entered a new phase of their histories, when the emphasis must be on building, on constructing, on developing, on healing—very much a *for* mode. You need new energy, a fresh vision, new insights.... What a privilege to be able to hand over this vibrant, tingling going concern to my successor. God be praised, for the Church belongs to God.[20]

By 1995, Tutu was very much looking forward to his retirement. His years as archbishop had been rewarding but exhausting. When Emory University in Atlanta invited him to return to their campus for a sabbatical following his retirement, he and Leah happily accepted.

Tutu had developed a loyal following during his 10 years as archbishop of Cape Town, both in South Africa and around the world. His closest aides often called him simply "the Arch." He even wore T-shirts emblazoned with that nickname. South Africa's Anglican bishops held a dinner in Tutu's honor shortly before his retirement. At the occasion, Bishop

Michael Nuttall, who as dean of the province called himself "number two to Tutu," made a surprise announcement. The bishops had decided to bestow upon Tutu a new title as of July 1, 1996—archbishop emeritus. The bestowal of such an unprecedented title left Tutu deeply moved. Usually archbishops became bishops again after retirement. The honorary title clearly illustrated the great esteem and affection with which the bishops regarded their leader.

On June 23, 1996, the Anglican Church held a farewell ceremony for Tutu at St. George's Cathedral. The audience included President Mandela; Deputy Presidents Mbeki and de Klerk; the presidents of Botswana and Mozambique; the king of Lesotho; the chief justice of South Africa; and family, friends, and admirers. The new archbishop of Canterbury, George Carey, gave the sermon. Bishop Nuttall offered a prayer of thanksgiving, saying, in part, "We thank you, God, for Desmond's ministry throughout the world, for hearts stirred and actions inspired, for hope restored and faith uplifted, for his commitment to peace and justice in the nearest and farthest corners of the earth, for his voice among the voiceless and marginalized."[21] President Mandela awarded Tutu South Africa's highest honor, the Order of Meritorious Service. After placing the medal on Tutu, Mandela warmly embraced his friend. The hundreds of guests gave Tutu a standing ovation. Tutu's eyes filled with tears as the applause thundered inside the ornate cathedral. His 10 years as archbishop of Cape Town had come to an end, but one more monumental task awaited him—a task as important as anything he had ever done before.

NOTES

1. Quoted in David Ottaway, *Chained Together: Mandela, De Klerk, and the Struggle to Remake South Africa* (New York: Times Books, 1993), p. 79.

2. Desmond Tutu, *The Rainbow People of God: The Making of a Peaceful Revolution*, ed. John Allen (New York: Doubleday, 1994), p. 192.

3. Tutu, *The Rainbow People of God*, p. 193.

4. Michael Nuttall, *Number Two to Tutu: A Memoir* (Pietermaritzburg: Cluster Publications, 2003), p. 72.

5. Tutu, *The Rainbow People of God*, pp. 196–97.

6. Tutu, *The Rainbow People of God*, p. 210.

7. Tutu, *The Rainbow People of God*, p. 212.

8. Tutu, *The Rainbow People of God*, p. 216.

9. Tutu, *The Rainbow People of God*, p. 229.

10. Desmond Tutu, "Momentous Choice, Without Us," *Los Angeles Times*, 20 March 1992.

11. Tutu, *The Rainbow People of God*, pp. 245–47.

12. "Tutu Urges Barring South Africa From the Olympics in Barcelona," *New York Times*, 23 June 1992.

13. Tutu, *The Rainbow People of God*, p. 256.

14. Adrian Hadland, *Desmond Tutu*, They Fought for Freedom Series (Cape Town: Maskew Miller Longman, 2001), p. 43.

15. Christopher Matthews, "The Prayers of Desmond Tutu," *San Francisco Examiner*, 1 May 1994 and "All Quiet in Town: Everyone Is Queuing to Vote," *Sydney Morning Herald*, 28 April 1994.

16. Tutu, *The Rainbow People of God*, pp. 263–64.

17. Tutu, *The Rainbow People of God*, pp. 268–69.

18. Nuttall, *Number Two to Tutu*, p. 135.

19. "Outcry Derails Gravy Train for S. African Officials," *Seattle Times*, 24 August 1994.

20. Nuttall, *Number Two to Tutu*, p. 139.

21. Nuttall, *Number Two to Tutu*, p. 152.

Chapter 14

TRUTH AND RECONCILIATION

In 1995, Nelson Mandela's government passed the Promotion of National Unity and Reconciliation Act. The law established a new organization in South Africa, the Truth and Reconciliation Commission. This commission would hear testimony from victims of apartheid-era human rights violations and offer amnesty to some human rights violators. The Truth and Reconciliation Commission (TRC) was founded on the premise that South Africans had to forgive each other for the hurtful actions of the past, so that citizens of all races could see each other as partners in the building of a new, united nation. If forgiveness was not forthcoming, simmering bitterness and resentment could explode into violence and destroy the fragile new nation.

When the law establishing the TRC was passed in 1995, Tutu and his wife were eagerly awaiting life outside the public spotlight after Desmond's retirement as archbishop of Cape Town. In mid-1995, Anglican Bishop Michael Nuttall suggested that Tutu accept nomination to the truth commission. Tutu initially declined, believing that it was time to give others the opportunity to serve. Later, he and Leah discussed the possibility between themselves, and Tutu eventually consented to be nominated. The Anglican bishops then unanimously sent Tutu's nomination to President Mandela in September 1995. Three months later, Tutu learned that he had been not only appointed to the TRC, but President Mandela wanted him to become the commission's chairperson. Tutu could not say no to his president. He agreed to serve, and thus had to postpone his sabbatical at Emory University—and his long-awaited retirement—for almost three years.

No one was more suited to lead the truth commission than Tutu. His uncompromising stand for justice and reconciliation and his unmatched integrity had brought him worldwide respect. Alex Boraine, the white South African who was appointed deputy chairperson of the TRC, believed Tutu was the ideal choice to lead the commission. Boraine later wrote,

> I don't think the Commission could have survived without the presence and person and leadership of Desmond Tutu. A Nobel Peace Prize Laureate and a tireless fighter for justice in South Africa, he was a household name long before he came to the Commission. He had demonstrated in his life and work an enormous compassion for the underdog. His sense of humor, his twinkling eyes, his tiny stature, his presence rather than his performance, meant that he was and is an icon in South Africa. His choice by President Mandela was an inspired one.[1]

Like the new government, Tutu and Boraine believed that South Africa needed to come to terms with its troubled past. Racial discrimination had become illegal in South Africa in 1994, but the shadow of apartheid did not dissipate overnight. Dark memories of violence, maltreatment, and discrimination still haunted South Africa. It was initially unclear how South Africans would deal with their past. During the negotiation process, the major parties ruled out Nuremberg-style tribunals (like those used to try Nazi war criminals after World War II) because neither side could claim absolute victory, as was the case after the Second World War. There had been a stalemate in South Africa; no one side could impose its will on the other without some form of compromise. Putting the old apartheid officials on trial was thus out of the question. The security forces would not have allowed the transition to continue had they faced the prospect of being put on trial afterward. As Tutu himself wrote, "There would have been no negotiated settlement and so no new democratic South Africa had the negotiators on one side insisted that all perpetrators be brought to trial. While the Allies could pack up and go home after Nuremberg, we in South Africa had to live with one another."[2]

Another option was to "let bygones be bygones," to forget the traumatic events of the past and grant all in the old regime a general amnesty. But forgetting the past would not work, according to Tutu, because the psychological scars were too deep. The new government wanted to expose past crimes so they would never happen again. Allowing victims to tell their stories in public might help them heal; it would also acknowledge their suffering in an important way. South Africa's truth and reconciliation process was thus a compromise between the punitive Nuremberg-style option and blanket amnesty. The South African option would offer the possibility of amnesty to those who fully confessed their human rights violations. If amnesty was granted, the applicant could not be prosecuted or sued for their past actions. The TRC's central role would thus be "to forgive rather than demand retribution."[3]

Amnesty would not be granted to all applicants automatically. To qualify for amnesty, several conditions had to be met. The act for which amnesty was sought had to have occurred between 1960 and 1994; the act must have been politically motivated; and the applicant must have made a full disclosure of the act. Applicants did not have to express remorse to receive amnesty. Furthermore, misdeeds committed by all sides would be considered, not just those committed by the apartheid government. Tutu believed that by offering amnesty for past human rights violations, the truth commission would promote "restorative justice" rather than "retributive justice." "The solution arrived at was not perfect," he admitted, "but it was the best that could be had in the circumstances—the truth in exchange for the freedom of the perpetrators."[4]

Tutu had long called for reconciliation and forgiveness in South Africa, even before the truth commission was devised. He believed that forgiveness involved forsaking the desire for revenge. In the best-case scenario, the victim would let go of his or her resentment, and the perpetrator would confess and express genuine remorse. "As Christians we are saying, 'Forgive one another as God in Christ forgave you.' That is the ideal we strive for," Tutu said.[5]

The truth and reconciliation process also required the South African government to offer reparations to victims of human rights abuses to further acknowledge their suffering. The TRC considered only gross human rights violations in its hearings, such as torture, killing, abduction, and assault. Covering all of the ill effects of apartheid (in the areas of health, education, and housing, for example) would have made the commission's task all but impossible.

During its nearly three years of full-time operations, the TRC would receive more than 7,000 applications for amnesty and hear testimony from approximately 2,500 victims. Almost 20,000 others submitted written statements. Tutu immersed himself in the "devastating but also exhilarating work of the commission, listening to the harrowing tales of horrendous atrocities and being uplifted by the extraordinary generosity of spirit of so many of our compatriots."[6] Tutu's position as chair of the TRC gave the commission immediate credibility with most black South Africans, who inherently trusted him. As one of Tutu's black colleagues on the TRC wrote, "For people burdened with the memory of a traumatic past, Archbishop Tutu's presence validated the pain they had suffered."[7]

The TRC met for the first time on December 16, 1995, at Tutu's residence at Bishopscourt. The day was a national holiday—the Day of Reconciliation. There were 17 commissioners in all, 10 men and 7 women. The racial breakdown was as follows: 7 Africans, 6 whites, 2 Indians, and 2 mixed-race South Africans. The group reflected the divisions of South African society, and unlike the Anglican bishops, the commissioners were not ready to accept Tutu's authority automatically. Tutu later acknowledged that meetings of the TRC could be "hell." The commission found it difficult to work as a team, especially at first. "We really were like a bunch of prima donnas, frequently hypersensitive, often taking umbrage easily at real or imagined slights," Tutu wrote. Once, when some commissioners questioned his integrity in a written statement, Tutu threatened to resign unless the statement was retracted. It was, but there were hurt feelings all around. "There were many moments when I thought I really should have my head examined for agreeing to take the job of chairing this particular commission," Tutu admitted later.[8]

Tutu found himself in the hot seat once again, just as he was supposed to be leaving it. He had to deal with a number of controversies before the TRC's work even got off the ground. Some black South Africans expressed dismay that the truth and reconciliation process would let perpetrators walk free. They feared that justice was missing from the commission's mandate. Many Afrikaners, on the other hand, thought that the TRC was designed to "denigrate their people."[9] The lack of white support would be an ongoing problem for the commission. Another controversy regarded Tutu's tendency to give the commission a semireligious character, even though the organization was a secular body. He opened meetings with prayers and wore his clerical robes at hearings. He regularly drew upon Christian teachings as he discussed the commission's work. Some objected to the religious character of the TRC, but Tutu viewed the commission's work as "profoundly religious and spiritual" because it dealt with healing and reconciliation.[10]

The TRC's first hearing began on April 16, 1996, at the East London city hall. Like many of the commission's hearings, it would be open to the public and partially broadcast on South African radio and television. The first hearing was set aside for victims. Tutu opened the occasion with a prayer. He asked God to comfort the victims, forgive the guilty, and help the commission reveal the truth and foster reconciliation. After his prayer, Tutu told those assembled, "We are charged to unearth the truth about our dark past; to lay the ghosts of the past so that they will not return to haunt us. And that we will thereby contribute to the healing of a traumatized and wounded people—for all of us in South Africa are wounded people—and in this manner to promote national unity and reconciliation."[11] As the hearing was getting under way, the TRC received a bomb threat, so the hall had to be evacuated and searched. No bomb was found, but the scare foreshadowed how controversial the truth and reconciliation process would become in the weeks and months ahead.

Toward the end of the hearing, a black South African described how he was tortured by South African police. Tutu was so overcome with emotion that he put his head down and began to weep. As he later recalled, "I could not hold back the tears. I just broke down and sobbed like a child. The floodgates opened. I bent over the table and covered my face with my hands. I told people afterward that I laugh easily and I cry easily and wondered whether I was the right person to lead the commission since I knew I was so weak and vulnerable."[12] Afterward, Tutu was mortified that the media had focused on his emotions rather than on the victims, so he steeled himself against public tears for the rest of the TRC hearings. He resolved to cry only at home or at church, but not at truth commission hearings.

Tutu and his fellow commissioners continued to hear graphic accounts of murder and torture that occurred during the apartheid era. Listening to so many terrible, heart-wrenching stories of suffering and loss took an emotional toll on Tutu. He felt overwhelmed by the depths of depravity to which some people sunk during the apartheid years. Sometimes Tutu became angry with God because so many suffered, but he never succumbed to bitterness. He weathered the pressures of leading the TRC by continuing his early morning prayers and meditation. He took daily Eucharist with his personal assistant, media secretary, and bodyguard. He was also comforted by the support and prayers from South Africans and the outside world. His work on the truth commission was not all grim, however. The commission reaffirmed Tutu's faith in humanity because many people demonstrated a remarkable capacity for good and a willingness to forgive. Some perpetrators redeemed themselves by showing real remorse for their actions. As Tutu frequently told his fellow commissioners, "There is no one who is devoid of possible redemption. We cannot give up on anyone."[13]

Some Afrikaners continued to accuse the TRC of being biased against them, but Tutu pledged that the commission would not vilify any particular group. He insisted that its mission was to expose past wrongs committed by all sides and to promote healing. Tutu often appealed to whites to support the TRC on radio talk shows, in newspaper columns, and at commission hearings. He believed that whites should welcome black ex-pressions of forgiveness and admit the role they played in supporting apartheid. At a TRC hearing in Paarl in October 1996, Tutu told the au-dience, "I want to say to the white community: you don't know how lucky you are that people are willing to forgive. All these people want is—not to put you in jail—but for people to come forward and say, 'We are sorry for what we did.'"[14] At that hearing, three white ministers from the Dutch Reformed Church in Stellenbosch publicly apologized for their church's support of apartheid. After their statements, Tutu got up from his chair-man's seat and embraced all three men.

Other whites continued to criticize the truth commission. Some even called it the "Kleenex commission" because it resulted in so many tears and tales of woe. As one white resident of Johannesburg said in 1996, "A lot of money is being wasted crying and screaming. It's not bringing back lives. I was a victim too—I had to go into the army against my will. I'm not standing there crying. The black man feels we owe him something, just because his skin is black."[15] Some whites were so angry at the truth commission that they made death threats to Tutu and other commission-ers. Tutu wished that more whites would display the same generosity of spirit as had President Mandela and many black South Africans.

Although Tutu was disturbed by victims' stories of anguish and suffer-ing, he marveled at how many were willing to forgive. Many victims were not consumed by hate. A white man blinded by an ANC bombing in Pre-toria (1983) expressed forgiveness to an activist who helped plan the at-tack. The daughter of a black activist killed by police in the eastern Cape (1984) was equally forgiving; so was a white man whose 8-year-old son was killed by an ANC bomb (1985); so were members of a black commu-nity in KwaZulu-Natal who lost relatives in a massacre organized by the South African police (1988). Tutu believed that these examples of for-giveness—and many others—showed that enemies could become friends and that both victims and perpetrators could heal.[16] Of course, not all vic-tims were so forgiving. The family of Steve Biko, for example, opposed amnesty for the policemen who killed their husband and father in 1977. When the alleged killers were denied amnesty, the Biko family considered pressing charges in court.

One of the key accomplishments of the TRC was that it helped un-cover the truth about past misdeeds that had been shrouded in mystery. The origins of the 1988 Khotso House bombing were revealed at hearings in 1996. Former Minister of Law and Order Adrian Vlok testified that P. W. Botha had ordered the bombing, not the ANC, as the government had suggested at the time. The culprits of other unsolved murders, disappearances, and bombings were revealed at other truth commission hearings.

In the midst of his work on the TRC, Tutu was diagnosed with prostate cancer. He had part of his prostate removed in January 1997 and remained in a Cape Town hospital for several days. He needed three weeks of recuperation before he could rejoin the commission. When his cancer was announced, Tutu received many messages of support, even from those who had probably considered him enemy number one in the past. For the next year, Tutu received medical treatment while he continued his work on the TRC. He traveled to the United States in March 1997 to receive medical advice at Johns Hopkins University Hospital. He had more consultations in New York. After returning to South Africa, he underwent three months of hormone treatment in Cape Town. He then began two months of radiation therapy at the Memorial Sloan-Kettering Cancer Center in New York. He underwent more outpatient radiation therapy in October 1997.

Throughout his ordeal, Tutu remained in good spirits. He exercised on a treadmill regularly and sought to remain active. He associated his illness with the burdens that he and his fellow commissioners bore as they tried to help heal a nation. Their work was not trivial, but it was difficult and sometimes traumatic. Tutu decided to publicize his disease to encourage men to have regular prostate exams. He was neither bitter nor fearful, despite his cancer diagnosis. As he told *Ebony* magazine, "Yes, it would be nice to stick around a little longer. But I believe as a Christian that death is the end of one part, but the beginning of another. It's like a doorway passing from one room of God's wonderful world to another."[17] Because of his cancer, Tutu could have withdrawn entirely from the TRC. He could have let someone else take over and gone into seclusion with his family. But he pressed on trying to heal the nation's wounds, despite needing time to heal himself.

One of the most difficult issues facing Tutu—besides his health—was how the TRC should deal with P. W. Botha, the state president of South Africa during the height of repression in the 1980s. After the truth commission learned that Botha had ordered the bombing of Khotso House, Tutu's deputy, Alex Boraine, suggested that Tutu visit Botha at his home in George to convince him to participate in the TRC process. Botha had withdrawn from public life but had gone on record as opposing the establishment of the truth commission. He also refused to apply for amnesty. As Tutu headed to George in late 1996, he remembered his tense encounters with Botha in the 1980s. This time their meeting was surprisingly cordial. In response to Tutu's overture, Botha agreed to supply written responses to TRC questions. To show that he harbored no grudges toward Botha, Tutu even returned to George to attend the funeral of Botha's wife. Tutu hoped that his presence would be interpreted as a goodwill gesture not only to P. W. Botha, but to Afrikaners in general.

The goodwill did not last. The truth commission eventually requested that Botha attend a hearing so that he could answer questions in person. When Botha refused, he was subpoenaed to appear at a hearing in October 1997. He chose not to attend and was duly charged with ignoring a legally binding TRC subpoena. Tutu wanted to avoid bringing Botha to trial, so he continued to encourage Botha's cooperation. He said that Botha could testify for only one day, in a hotel in George, with questions in advance, and with his doctor present (Botha's health was failing as he aged and he had suffered a stroke eight years earlier). According to Tutu, the TRC bent over backward to accommodate Botha's needs.[18] Some black South Africans accused the commission of treating Botha too deferentially, but Botha still refused to cooperate. He was then formally charged with refusing to comply with the TRC's subpoena. At Botha's trial in February 1998, Tutu urged his old nemesis to apologize for the pain his government's policies had caused. Botha's only reply was silence. The presiding judge found Botha guilty, but the conviction was later set aside on a technicality. Despite Tutu's best efforts to elicit a statement of regret from Botha, the aging ex-leader was unrepentant.

Tutu also hoped that Botha's successor, F. W. de Klerk, would cooperate with the truth commission. De Klerk agreed to testify but refused to take responsibility for any of the human rights violations that occurred during his time in office. At his appearance before the TRC in May 1997, de Klerk testified that the National Party government never endorsed torture, murder, or other human rights violations. Tutu listened in disbelief and publicly questioned whether de Klerk was being truthful. De Klerk then asked Tutu to apologize. When Tutu refused, de Klerk filed a lawsuit against the TRC and withdrew the National Party from the whole truth and reconciliation process. Tutu wanted to avoid a court battle, so he authorized a lawyer to apologize on his behalf in September 1997. De Klerk dropped the lawsuit a few weeks later, but he never applied for amnesty and never fully apologized. Tutu remained troubled by de Klerk's refusal to take responsibility for the actions of his security forces during South Africa's turbulent negotiation process.

Another well-known South African political leader generated controversy at the TRC—Winnie Madikizela-Mandela, the ex-wife of Nelson
Mandela. (The Mandelas divorced in 1996.) Winnie's bodyguards in
Soweto, known colloquially as the "Mandela United Football Club," had
terrorized local residents in the late 1980s by assaulting and sometimes
killing those they suspected of being collaborators with apartheid authorities. In 1991, Winnie had been convicted of kidnapping and assaulting a
14-year-old local activist, Stompie Seipei, who was found dead in early
1989. The truth commission held nine days of hearings on Winnie's "football club." During these hearings, several people testified that Winnie had
ordered her followers to commit assault and murder. The former head of
her security detail said she personally authorized the murder of young
Stompie. The TRC subpoenaed Winnie to hear her side of the story.

Tutu was in an awkward position during these hearings. He had long
admired Winnie as "the Mother of the Nation," as had many black South
Africans. She had suffered banishment, banning, and detention while her
husband Nelson was in prison. Despite the repression, she had boldly spoken out against apartheid and gained a national following, especially
among poor, disaffected black youths from the townships. During Winnie's years of exile in Brandfort, almost 500 miles from her home in
Soweto, Tutu sometimes helped Winnie celebrate the Eucharist. Their
families lived in the same neighborhood in Soweto, Orlando West. Winnie's daughters even called Tutu "uncle." In short, Tutu greatly admired
Winnie's contribution to the antiapartheid struggle, but he was wary of
appearing to excuse her misdeeds.

Winnie appeared before the TRC in November 1997. She was evasive
throughout the hearing, dodging some questions and dismissing all of the
charges against her as "ludicrous." On the ninth and last day of the hearings, Tutu noted how close his family was to the Mandelas and then spoke
directly to Winnie:

> There are people out there who want to embrace you. I still em-
> brace you because I love you and I love you very deeply.... I beg
> you, I beg you, I beg you, please. I have not made any particular
> finding from what has happened here. I speak as someone who
> has lived in this community. You are a great person and you
> don't know how your greatness would be enhanced if you were
> to say sorry, things went wrong, forgive me. I beg you.[19]

Winnie then admitted that things had gone wrong, but she did not take
personal responsibility for those things. Her apology was halfhearted at

best. After the hearing, Tutu was criticized in the media for treating Winnie too deferentially. Even TRC deputy chair Alex Boraine believed that Tutu could have been "more circumspect and more judicial" during the hearing. "He cared so deeply that he did not contemplate for a moment the misconceptions that could ensue," Boraine later wrote.[20] The truth commission's final report indicated that Winnie had been involved in assaults, cover-ups, and attempted murder, most of which were linked to her bodyguards.

The TRC continued to make headlines after the controversy surrounding Winnie had dissipated. In June 1998, the truth commission uncovered details about the apartheid government's secret chemical and biological weapons program. Undercover agents had tried to kill SACC General Secretary Frank Chikane in the late 1980s by poisoning his clothing. The government had also developed a secret research program to reduce the black birthrate and had considered introducing drugs into black South African communities to undermine morale. Government agents had even considered poisoning Nelson Mandela in the 1980s while he was still in prison.

Tutu was horrified by all of these revelations. He was invited to preach at a Dutch Reformed Church in Pretoria just after the secret weapons hearings ended. Several members of the church he visited had served in the old government, so Tutu understandably felt as if he were going into the "lion's den."[21] But he received a warm welcome. In his sermon, he urged Afrikaners to embrace the new dispensation and to become part of it. He hoped someone would express remorse for the government's chemical warfare program. After he finished speaking, one of the church's Afrikaner ministers arose unexpectedly, walked over to Tutu, and said, "As a minister of the Dutch Reformed Church for twenty years, as a chaplain in the defense force, I want to say to you we are sorry. For what we have done wrong we ask for forgiveness."[22] As the speaker choked back tears, Tutu stood up and embraced him. Then the congregation gave the two clerics a standing ovation. Tutu felt God's hand at work in this memorable moment of forgiveness and reconciliation.

Tutu participated in another moving occasion a few weeks later. On July 18, 1998, Nelson Mandela celebrated his 80th birthday by marrying Graca Machel of Mozambique at his home in Johannesburg. Tutu attended the ceremony with a handful of other guests, including one of Mandela's former prison guards from Robben Island. After Nelson and Graca exchanged rings, Tutu and Methodist bishop Mvume Dandala offered their blessings. Tutu quipped, "The Garden of Eden was alright before woman arrived, but it was even better after."[23]

As the TRC prepared to issue its final report in October 1998, yet another controversy erupted. One the eve of the report's publication, the ANC requested a last-minute meeting to discuss the report's coverage of its own human rights violations. Some commissioners wanted to agree to the meeting, but this would have violated the TRC's own operating procedures. Tutu believed that to accede to such a request would open the truth commission to accusations that it was biased in favor of the ANC, an accusation he had denied ever since the TRC was established. He feared such a move would destroy the commission's credibility. When the TRC became deadlocked over whether to consider the ANC's objections, Tutu cast the deciding vote against doing so. Then the ANC filed a motion in court to prevent publication of parts of the report until the TRC considered its appeal. The ANC argued that because the report discussed its human rights violations, it wrongly put the liberation movement on equal footing with the apartheid government, which also violated human rights. Tutu disagreed. "We may say that the fact of opposing apartheid put people on a higher moral plane than someone who justified and maintained it, but that does not mean that any act committed in a just cause is morally acceptable."[24]

Tutu was dismayed by the ANC's actions because it had fully supported the TRC's procedures from the start. The ANC had not only revealed its violations, it had also apologized for them. A court dismissed the ANC's motion, but Tutu remained deeply troubled by the organization's eleventh-hour attempt to delay the report and squelch criticism of its past misdeeds. Would the ANC government take action against its critics in the future? Not if Tutu could help it. "I have struggled against a tyranny. I did not do that in order to substitute another," he said. "If there is a tyranny or an abuse of power, let them know that I will oppose it with every fiber of my being. That is who I am."[25]

F. W. de Klerk also filed a brief, demanding that references to him be stricken from the TRC report. A judge accepted his position, greatly disappointing Tutu. Sections on de Klerk had to be blacked out until the matter was settled in court.

Tutu finally presented the five-volume TRC report to President Mandela at a public ceremony in Pretoria on October 29, 1998. The occasion was bittersweet because of the last-minute legal challenges and the fact that the major political parties (ANC, National Party, and Inkatha Freedom Party) boycotted the event amid accusations that the TRC was biased against them. As he handed the report to Mandela, Tutu said, "We have looked the beast in the eye. Our past will no longer keep us hostage.

We who are the rainbow people of God will hold hands together and say: never again, nooit weer, ngekhe futhi, ga reno tlola."[26] (The last three phrases mean "never again" in Afrikaans, Zulu, and Sotho.) The report labeled apartheid a crime against humanity, but it also criticized liberation groups for human rights violations during the antiapartheid struggle. Mandela reacted to the report's findings a few days later: "As a man who read the report and set up the commission and has the highest respect not only for Archbishop Tutu but all the commissioners, I am satisfied they have done a good job, even if there are imperfections."[27]

According to a 1998 poll, most South Africans believed that the truth and reconciliation process had worsened racial tensions in South Africa, at least temporarily. Tutu was not surprised. He insisted that reconciliation would take time and that it could not succeed if the truth remained buried. He believed it was unrealistic to expect that racial tensions that had built up for centuries would completely vanish in a few years.

From Tutu's vantage point, the TRC had been a highly worthwhile enterprise. He felt awed by the many instances of forgiveness and reconciliation between perpetrators and victims, which he believed boded well for South Africa's future. He was grateful that a number of policemen applied for amnesty and thereby revealed information about disappearances and unsolved murders during the apartheid era. And he was proud that the TRC had given people the opportunity to tell their stories and, in so doing, begin to heal. But Tutu wasn't blind to the shortcomings of the truth and reconciliation process. He was troubled that the government took so long to approve reparations, which he believed only prolonged the suffering of the victims. He regretted that relatively few whites had embraced the truth commission and that so few political leaders applied for amnesty. Tutu realized that the TRC process was imperfect but believed that it ultimately did much to reveal the truth and promote reconciliation. It provided a way for former adversaries to live together after a prolonged period of conflict and division.

Tutu was convinced that true reconciliation could only occur if the gap between the rich and the poor was reduced in South Africa. "For unless houses replace the hovels and shacks in which most blacks live, unless blacks gain access to clean water, electricity, affordable health care, decent education, good jobs, and a safe environment—things which the vast majority of whites have taken for granted for so long—we can just as well kiss reconciliation goodbye," he wrote.[28] From Tutu's perspective, reconciliation could not be achieved overnight. It was an ongoing process that required effort by all.

NOTES

1. Alex Boraine, *A Country Unmasked: Inside South Africa's Truth and Reconciliation Commission* (Cape Town: Oxford University Press, 2000), p. 268.

2. Desmond Tutu, *No Future Without Forgiveness* (New York: Doubleday, 1999), p. 21.

3. Tutu, *No Future Without Forgiveness*, p. 31.

4. Tutu, *No Future Without Forgiveness*, p. 58.

5. *Archbishop Desmond Tutu with Bill Moyers*, VHS (Princeton, NJ: Films for the Humanities and Sciences, 1999).

6. Tutu, *No Future Without Forgiveness*, p. 69.

7. Pumla Gobodo-Madikizela, *A Human Being Died That Night: A South African Story of Forgiveness* (Boston: Houghton Mifflin, 2003), p. 81.

8. Tutu, *No Future Without Forgiveness*, pp. 195–96.

9. Erna Paris, *Long Shadows: Truth, Lies and History* (New York: Bloomsbury, 2001), p. 279.

10. Tutu, *No Future Without Forgiveness*, p. 82 and Boraine, *A Country Unmasked*, p. 262.

11. Tutu, *No Future Without Forgiveness*, p. 114.

12. Tutu, *No Future Without Forgiveness*, p. 144.

13. Boraine, *A Country Unmasked*, p. 262.

14. David Goodman, *Fault Lines: Journeys into the New South Africa* (Berkeley: University of California Press, 1999), p. 197.

15. Quoted in Tina Rosenberg, "Recovering from Apartheid," *New Yorker*, 18 November 1996, p. 93.

16. Tutu, *No Future Without Forgiveness*, p. 158.

17. "Desmond Tutu: 'There's Life after Prostate Cancer,'" *Ebony*, February 1998, pp. 166–68.

18. Tutu, *No Future Without Forgiveness*, p. 248.

19. Lynne Duke, *Mandela, Mobutu, and Me: A Newswoman's African Journey* (New York: Doubleday, 2003), p. 207.

20. Boraine, *A Country Unmasked*, pp. 252–53.

21. Tutu, *No Future Without Forgiveness*, p. 184.

22. Allister Sparks, *Beyond the Miracle: Inside the New South Africa* (Chicago: University of Chicago Press, 2003), p. 169.

23. "Madiba Turns 80, Then He and Graca Say I Do, I Do," *Sunday Argus* (Cape Town), 18/19 July 1998.

24. Paris, *Long Shadows*, p. 280.

25. "S. African Report Draws Bitterness," *Washington Post*, 30 October 1998.

26. Adrian Hadland, *Desmond Tutu*, They Fought for Freedom Series (Cape Town: Maskew Miller Longman, 2001), p. 48.

27. Boraine, *A Country Unmasked*, p. 317.

28. Tutu, *No Future Without Forgiveness*, p. 274.

Chapter 15

TOO BUSY TO RETIRE

Tutu was 67 years old when he presented the truth commission's report to President Nelson Mandela in October 1998. After the arduous work of the TRC, Tutu finally got the chance to enjoy his long-awaited retirement. But he had no intention of slowing down.

From the late 1990s on, Tutu spoke to audiences all over the world about South Africa's transition from apartheid to democracy. One of his constant themes was that South Africa could be a model for the rest of the world, both in terms of its conflict resolution and its truth and reconciliation process. Tutu wanted the world to realize that there was no situation that was beyond hope. "God wants to point to us as a possible beacon of hope, a possible paradigm, and to say, 'Look at South Africa. They had a nightmare called apartheid. It has ended. Northern Ireland (or wherever), your nightmare will end too. They had a problem regarded as intractable. They are resolving it. No problem anywhere can ever again be considered to be intractable. There is hope for you too.'"[1] In 1998 Tutu visited Dublin and Belfast. In his speeches he used the South African example to show that even the seemingly insurmountable problems of a society could be resolved. Catastrophe could be averted. As he later wrote, "The death and resurrection of Jesus Christ puts the issue beyond doubt: ultimately goodness and laughter and peace and compassion and gentleness and forgiveness and reconciliation will have the last word and prevail over their ghastly counterparts. The victory over apartheid was proof positive of the truth of this seemingly utopian dream."[2]

Tutu also traveled around the United States, thanking American college students and others for supporting South Africa's freedom struggle. In his view, their support of sanctions and disinvestment helped end apartheid. He told his audiences, "We are free because of you. Our victory over apartheid would not have happened without you."[3] Tutu also believed that just as Europe needed a Marshall plan to recover from the devastation of World War II, southern Africa needed a Marshall plan to recover from the devastation of apartheid. He frequently called for more American investment in South Africa. "We hope that our friends who listened to us when we said 'divest' will now listen to us when we say 'invest,'" he told reporters.[4]

Tutu spoke out publicly in the months after the terrorist attacks of September 11, 2001. In a lecture at Georgetown University in November 2001, he noted that as the world's only superpower, the United States had the greatest military might, but he argued that Americans should measure their greatness in terms of moral stature, not military strength. He called on the United States to share its wealth and values and shun policies that might cause harm or suffering. He concluded by outlining what he saw as God's dream for the world:

> You and I are made for goodness, for love, for transcendence, for togetherness. God has a dream that we, God's children, will come to realize that we are indeed sisters and brothers, members of one family, God's family, the human family—that all belong, all white, black and yellow, rich and poor, beautiful and not so beautiful, young and old, male and female, there are no outsiders, all, all are insiders—gay and straight, Christians, Muslims, Jews, Arabs, Americans, Protestants, Roman Catholics, Afghans, all, all belong. And God says, "I have no one to help me realize my dream except you—will you help me?"[5]

The idea that "God has a dream" became one of Tutu's favorite themes as the twenty-first century dawned.

Tutu not only lectured all over the world, but he also accepted offers to teach whenever he could. He was a visiting professor at the Candler School of Theology at Emory University in Atlanta from 1998 to 2000. There he taught, gave public lectures and interviews, participated in religious services on campus, and wrote *No Future Without Forgiveness*, an account of his experiences on the Truth and Reconciliation Commission. When he returned to South Africa, Tutu denied rumors that he intended to settle permanently in the United States. "Home is here, this is a great country," he insisted.[6] Following his two years at Emory, Tutu began a new pattern of accepting visiting professorships overseas during the first half of each year and then returning home to South Africa for the second half of the year. He taught at the Episcopal Divinity School in Cambridge, Massachusetts, during the first half of 2002. From January to May 2003, he was a visiting scholar-in-residence at the University of North Florida in Jacksonville, where he taught a course on South Africa's truth and reconciliation process. He accepted a position as visiting professor of postconflict societies at King's College, University of London, beginning in January 2004. Tutu had fond memories of King's College, where he received his bachelor's and master's degrees in divinity in the 1960s.

Even as he lectured and taught overseas, Tutu knew that his permanent legacy rested in South Africa. He and his friends and supporters began to make plans for an institute bearing his name that would give future generations the opportunity to reflect on his ideas. The Desmond Tutu Peace Centre was publicly launched on June 15, 2000, at the South African consulate in New York. The center, based in Cape Town, was designed to honor those who have worked for peace in South Africa and promote the development of young leaders. Plans for the center included a library and archive holding Tutu's personal papers, an interactive museum, and a leadership program. Nelson Mandela actively supported the center's establishment. In a letter endorsing the center, Mandela wrote, "[Tutu's] contribution to the transition of South Africa to democracy, the reconciliation of her people through the pursuit of truth and the example of his own life has been and remains an inspiration to us all."[7] The peace center's Emerging Leadership Program got off the ground in 2003. Tutu awarded 20 young South Africans medals and certificates at a ceremony in Cape Town in recognition of their involvement in community projects, such as those to combat drugs, crime, and AIDS and to promote academic achievement and musical performance.

Bishop Michael Nuttall, Tutu's former "number two" in the Anglican Church in South Africa, recognized a supreme irony about Tutu. Although he had been demonized by the SABC and many white Anglicans during the 1980s, he had become one of South Africa's most admired elder statesmen after the fall of apartheid. Many schools and scholarships now bear Tutu's name. The Archbishop Desmond Mpilo Tutu Heritage Centre opened in Klerksdorp, Tutu's birthplace, in 2000. That same year, the Munsieville Library in Krugersdorp was renamed the Desmond Tutu Library. (Tutu had lived in Munsieville as a teenager and young teacher.) The Desmond Tutu School of Theology was dedicated at Fort Hare University in 2002. (Tutu had served as the Anglican chaplain at Fort Hare in the late 1960s.) Tutu also continued to receive many international awards and honorary degrees, especially in South Africa, Britain, and the United

States. By 2003, he had been awarded approximately 100 honorary degrees worldwide.

Despite his many honors, Tutu was not yet ready to be a museum piece.
He still had a burning desire to speak out on issues of peace and politics.
He became particularly troubled as tension increased between the United
States and Iraq in early 2003. During an appearance on British television
on January 5, 2003, Tutu said he was "deeply saddened" by the prospect of
a U.S.-led invasion of Iraq. "The United States should not seek to go it
alone," he said. "One of the wonderful things about this country, it promoted respect for the rule of law, for international law."[8] He believed that
the international community should cooperate on a strategy regarding
Iraq. On February 15, 2003, simultaneous demonstrations against a possible invasion of Iraq were held in Berlin, London, Madrid, New York,
Paris, Rome, and elsewhere. Tutu participated in the antiwar demonstration in New York. During a protest near the UN headquarters, Tutu
shouted, "Peace! Peace! Peace!" and urged the United States to listen to
world opinion and refrain from going to war. U.S. television news programs broadcast images of Tutu as animated as ever, telling a crowd that a
war without provocation was immoral. Tutu's participation in the antiwar
protest left him feeling invigorated. He drew strength from the display of
"people power" demonstrating for peace.[9]

The American-led coalition invaded Iraq in March 2003. Two months
later, Tutu gave the commencement address at the University of Pennsyl-
vania in Philadelphia. During his remarks, he stressed the need for countries to use peaceful means to solve international problems, just as the
United States did to help end apartheid. He told the audience, "You in
this country helped us to become free. You helped us to become democratic. You helped us to become a country that is seeking to be nonracial
and nonsexist. You didn't bomb us into liberation. We became free nonviolently. And the country demonstrated that there are other ways of
dealing with difference, with disagreement, with conflict: the way of forgiveness, the way of compromise, the way of reconciliation."[10] Most ap-
plauded Tutu's remarks, but when Tutu said that peace in the Middle East
depended on the establishment of a Palestinian state, some in the audience booed. Some families had boycotted Tutu's speech, accusing him of
being anti-Israeli, while others were glad he had been invited to speak.

As the war in Iraq was beginning, Tutu presented the final two volumes
of the TRC report to President Thabo Mbeki during a low-key ceremony
in Pretoria on March 21, 2003 (Mandela had retired as president in
1999). The final report said that former President F. W. de Klerk had
"knowingly withheld information from the commission about state-

sponsored [human rights] violations."[11] These findings had been blacked out from the report in 1998 because of de Klerk's legal challenge. The final report also charged Mangosuthu Buthelezi's Inkatha Freedom Party with collaborating with the white right in attacks in the early 1990s. Volume seven of the report summarized the testimony of victims who gave evidence to the truth commission. As it published its final report, the TRC urged the government to speed up reparation payments to victims. Tutu recommended that the government impose a new tax on businesses to help pay for reparations.

In April 2003, President Mbeki announced that the government planned to pay the equivalent of $3,900 to each of the thousands of victims who testified before the TRC. Like most aspects of the truth commission, the figure was controversial. The TRC had requested reparation payments totaling $360 million, while the government agreed to payments totaling $85 million. The government rejected Tutu's proposal that businesses be taxed to help pay for reparations. Some black South Africans believed that the reparation figures were far too low. Although the controversies surrounding the truth commission would live on, Tutu's work on the commission had come to an end.

As the 10th anniversary of South Africa's first democratic elections approached, Tutu still looked back on the fall of apartheid with a sense of wonder. "When shackles are removed from you, it's something you'll never forget. It's unrepeatable. It's difficult to describe. It's as difficult as describing a Beethoven symphony to a deaf man," he said.[12] Tutu believed that South Africa was remarkably stable after 1994, given its many races, ethnic groups, and languages. In his view, the country could have easily gone the way of Yugoslavia and fractured along ethnic lines after years of repressive rule. He was overjoyed at the progress South Africa had made. "It's fantastic to look at schools today that were segregated just ten years ago and to see children who were made to be enemies by government decree now playing together," he said.[13] From Tutu's perspective, a large part of South Africa's success was due to Nelson Mandela. Tutu regularly paid tribute to the towering leadership of South Africa's first black president, who had emerged from almost 30 years in prison filled not with bitterness, but with a spirit of true reconciliation.

Tutu recognized that South Africa faced tremendous challenges. Some old racial attitudes persisted, and most blacks remained mired in poverty. The divisions of the past would not disappear overnight. Tutu hoped that South Africa would continue to recognize the diversity of its citizens but give everyone equal rights, freedoms, and opportunities. He viewed AIDS, poverty, and crime as South Africa's most serious problems. During an SABC interview in 2001, Tutu said that South Africa needed to get more serious about fighting AIDS. "Let's stop playing marbles and roll up our sleeves and invoke the spirit that inspired all of us to win the struggle against apartheid," he said.[14] The South African government had been criticized both at home and abroad for not doing enough to prevent and treat the disease. Of 42 million people with AIDS in the world, 29 million lived in sub-Saharan Africa, and South Africa had more AIDS victims than any other African country. Tutu was committed to speaking out about the epidemic. He attended a news conference in Beverly Hills, California, in June 2003 in which plans were launched for a concert tour benefiting AIDS programs in South Africa. "Apartheid tried to destroy our people and apartheid failed. If we don't act against HIV-AIDS, it may succeed, for it is already decimating our population," he said.[15] Tutu refused to keep silent about his country's other problems. At the funeral of ANC leader Walter Sisulu a month earlier, Tutu praised the high ideals of the antiapartheid movement but lamented rising crime and corruption in South Africa. Freedom fighters had not waged the struggle so that carjackers, corrupt officials, and abusers of women and children could run rampant, he told the mourners. Notwithstanding his concerns, Tutu remained generally optimistic about South Africa's future prospects. "I think we are going to make it," he said. "The world needs a South Africa that has succeeded."[16] And South Africa still needed him.

Despite his cancer diagnosis of January 1997, Tutu hoped to be around for a long time. According to the World Health Organization, 89 percent of men diagnosed with prostate cancer survive at least 5 years; 63 percent survive at least 10 years.[17] Tutu had minor surgery at Emory University Hospital in October 1999 to determine if his cancer had spread beyond the prostate; doctors reported that it had not. A month later, Tutu underwent a procedure known as cryosurgery, in which cancerous tissue is frozen to destroy cancer cells. The procedure went well, and afterward Leah was by Tutu's side to offer comfort and support. In October 2000, a South African newspaper reported that Tutu's doctors in Cape Town had pronounced him clear of prostate cancer. When he appeared on SABC television to mark his 70th birthday on October 7, 2001, Tutu said that he felt good, despite his bout with cancer. He underwent another round of prostate surgery in April 2003 from which he seemed to recover quickly.

Tutu remained in good spirits despite his ongoing medical treatment. When American journalist Bill Moyers asked about his health in 1999, Tutu chuckled, "There's life after cancer." As he told Moyers, so many of his friends had prayed for his health that God said, " 'The only way to deal with all these prayers is to get him well.'"[18] Tutu didn't bargain with God for more time. He looked back on his life with a sense of gratitude. In particular, he derived enormous satisfaction at having been part of the successful struggle to end apartheid. His illness also gave him a new appreciation for life. Of his cancer, he said,

> It helps concentrate your mind. There is not enough time to be nasty. Things that you have taken for granted—the love of your family and friends, lovely moments with your grandchildren, the beauty of God's creation, the flowers—they are the same things you saw yesterday, but now they have a different intensity. There comes the time when your relationship with God becomes much clearer. Everything is a gift. Life is a gift.[19]

Tutu faced the future not with fear, but with his characteristic zest for life, sense of humor, and commitment to peace and reconciliation. His faith in God's dream remained undiminished.

NOTES

1. Desmond Tutu, *No Future Without Forgiveness* (New York: Doubleday, 1999), p. 282.

2. Tutu, *No Future Without Forgiveness*, p. 267.

3. *Archbishop Desmond Tutu with Bill Moyers*, VHS (Princeton, NJ: Films for the Humanities and Sciences, 1999).

4. "Tutu: America Led Way for His Nation," *Birmingham News*, 19 April 2002.

5. "Archbishop Tutu's Message to America," *Sunday Independent*, 4 November 2001.

6. "We Can Overcome Our Problems: Tutu," *ANC Daily News Briefing*, 9 October 2001.

7. Nelson Mandela to Chris Ahrends, 12 December 2001, Desmond Tutu Peace Centre home page, www.tutu.org.

8. "Tutu Calls on Bush to Work with U.N. on Iraq," *Jacksonville.com*, 8 January 2003, www.jacksonville.com/tu-online/stories/010803/met_11414418.shtml.

9. "Protesters around Globe Voice Opposition to War," *Montgomery Advertiser*, 16 February 2003 and "It's Wonderful to Be Alive at a Moment Like This," *Minneapolis Star Tribune*, 26 February 2003.

10. "Reflections on War, Peace, and How to Live Vitally and Act Globally," *New York Times*, 1 June 2003.

11. "South African Commission Ends Its Work," *New York Times*, 22 March 2003.

12. Desmond Tutu, in discussion with the author, 29 April 2003, Jacksonville, FL.

13. "Tutu: America Led Way for His Nation."

14. "We Can Overcome Our Problems: Tutu," ANC Daily News Briefing, 9 October 2001.

15. "Grammy Winner Plans Tour Fund-Raiser for AIDS," Montgomery Advertiser, 7 June 2003.

16. Allister Sparks, Beyond the Miracle: Inside the New South Africa (Chicago: University of Chicago Press, 2003), p. 330.

17. "Mandela Battles Cancer," Cape Argus (Cape Town), 24 July 2001.

18. Archbishop Desmond Tutu with Bill Moyers, VHS (Princeton, NJ: Films for the Humanities and Sciences, 1999).

19. Adrian Hadland, Desmond Tutu, They Fought for Freedom Series (Cape Town: Maskew Miller Longman, 2001), p. 49.

GLOSSARY

Afrikaans—language spoken by the descendants of early Dutch, French, and German settlers; also widely spoken by mixed-race South Africans.

ANC—African National Congress; antiapartheid organization founded in 1912; became the new governing party of South Africa after the first democratic elections in 1994.

Apartheid—the legalized system of racial discrimination that severely limited the rights and opportunities of the black majority in South Africa (implemented in 1948 and dismantled by 1994); "apartheid" means "apartness" or "separateness" in Afrikaans.

Archbishop of Canterbury—the highest official in the worldwide Anglican Church; based in Britain.

AZAPO—Azanian People's Organization; antiapartheid organization founded in 1978.

Bantu education—system of black education implemented by the apartheid government in the mid-1950s that stressed vocational training and manual labor rather than academic subjects.

Basotho people—residents of Lesotho.

Disinvestment—withdrawal of investment from a country or company.

Eucharist—an act of worship during which bread and wine are consumed to commemorate the death of Jesus Christ.

Fed Sem—Federal Theological Seminary in Alice, eastern Cape, South Africa.

Inkatha—a Zulu cultural organization that became a political party (the Inkatha Freedom Party) in 1990 under the leadership of Mangosuthu Buthelezi.

Khotso House—building in central Johannesburg that served as headquarters of the South African Council of Churches and other antiapartheid organizations; literally, "house of peace."

Mpilo—"life" or "live" in the Xhosa language; can also mean "health"; Tutu's middle name.

PAC—Pan Africanist Congress; antiapartheid organization founded in 1959.

Pass laws—laws requiring black South Africans to carry identity documents known as passes at all times in order to travel, seek work, and find housing.

SABC—South African Broadcasting Corporation.

SACC—South African Council of Churches; interdenominational Christian organization that opposed apartheid.

Soweto—network of black townships southwest of Johannesburg with a population of at least two million; acronym for South Western Townships.

Synod—an assembly of church officials.

TEF—Theological Education Fund; a London-based branch of the World Council of Churches that supports theological education in Asia, Africa, and Latin America; established in 1958.

TRC—Truth and Reconciliation Commission; body established in 1995 to probe past human rights abuses in South Africa and solicit testimony from perpetrators (who could apply for amnesty) and victims.

Ubuntu—an African concept of community spirit; literally, "a person is a person through other persons."

UDF—United Democratic Front; coalition of antiapartheid groups established in South Africa in 1983.

UNISA—University of South Africa, a Pretoria-based institution of higher education that conducts most of its courses by correspondence.

WCC—World Council of Churches; an organization that promotes international cooperation among Christian churches; established in 1948 and headquartered in Geneva, Switzerland.

Witwatersrand—Literally, "ridge of white waters"; the gold-rich territory of Johannesburg and the surrounding area.

WRAB—West Rand Administration Board; the government body that administered Soweto in the 1970s.

SELECTED BIBLIOGRAPHY

SELECTION OF PUBLISHED WORKS BY DESMOND TUTU

"Acceptance of the Nobel Peace Prize" and "Nobel Lecture." (10–11 December 1984.) In *Statements: Occasional Papers of the Phelps-Stokes Fund*, no. 1, Oslo, Norway, November 1986, pp. 27–39.

An African Prayer Book. New York: Doubleday, 1995.

Crying in the Wilderness: The Struggle for Justice in South Africa. Grand Rapids, MI: William B. Eerdmans, 1982. 3rd ed., 1990.

The Essential Desmond Tutu. Compiled by John Allen. Cape Town: David Philip, 1997.

God Has a Dream. New York: Doubleday, 2004.

Hope and Suffering: Sermons and Speeches. Grand Rapids, MI: William B. Eerdmans, 1984.

"Momentous Choice, Without Us." *Los Angeles Times*, 20 March 1992.

No Future Without Forgiveness. New York: Doubleday, 1999.

The Rainbow People of God: The Making of a Peaceful Revolution. Edited by John Allen. New York: Doubleday, 1994.

"The Question of South Africa." (Address to the UN Security Council, 23 October 1984.) In *The Global Experience: Readings in World History Since 1550*. Edited by Philip Riley and others, vol. 2, 4th ed., Upper Saddle River, NJ: Prentice Hall, 2002.

The Wisdom of Desmond Tutu. Compiled by Michael Battle. Louisville, KY: Westminster John Knox Press, 2000.

The Words of Desmond Tutu. Selected and introduced by Naomi Tutu. New York: Newmarket Press, 1989. Reprinted in 1996.

BOOKS

Anzovin, Steven, ed. *South Africa: Apartheid and Disinvestment, The Reference Shelf*. New York: H. W. Wilson, 1987.

Battle, Michael. *Reconciliation: The Ubuntu Theology of Desmond Tutu*. Cleveland: The Pilgrim Press, 1997.

Bentley, Judith. *Archbishop Tutu of South Africa*. Hillside, NJ: Enslow, 1988.

Bonner, Philip, and Lauren Segal. *Soweto: A History*. Cape Town: Maskew Miller Longman, 1998.

Boraine, Alex. *A Country Unmasked: Inside South Africa's Truth and Reconciliation Commission*. Cape Town: Oxford University Press, 2000.

Crocker, Chester A. *High Noon in Southern Africa: Making Peace in a Rough Neighborhood*. New York: W.W. Norton, 1992.

De Gruchy, John. *The Church Struggle in South Africa*. Grand Rapids, MI: William B. Eerdmans, 1986.

Du Boulay, Shirley. *Tutu: Voice of the Voiceless*. Grand Rapids, MI: William B. Eerdmans, 1988.

Duke, Lynne. *Mandela, Mobutu, and Me: A Newswoman's African Journey*. New York: Doubleday, 2003.

Gobodo-Madikizela, Pumla. *A Human Being Died That Night: A South African Story of Forgiveness*. Boston: Houghton Mifflin, 2003.

Goodman, David. *Fault Lines: Journeys into the New South Africa*. Berkeley: University of California Press, 1999.

Hadland, Adrian. *Desmond Tutu*. They Fought for Freedom Series. Cape Town: Maskew Miller Longman, 2001.

Honore, Deborah Duncan, ed. *Trevor Huddleston: Essays on His Life and Work*. New York: Oxford University Press, 1988.

Huddleston, Trevor. *Naught for Your Comfort*. Garden City, NY: Doubleday, 1956.

Hulley, Leonard, Louise Kretzschmar, and Luke Lungile Pato, eds. *Archbishop Tutu: Prophetic Witness in South Africa*. Cape Town: Human & Rousseau, 1996.

Koppel, Ted, and Kyle Gibson. *Nightline: History in the Making and the Making of Television*. New York: Times Books, 1996.

Massie, Robert Kinloch. *Loosing the Bonds: The United States and South Africa in the Apartheid Years*. New York: Nan A. Talese, 1997.

Mufson, Steven. *Fighting Years: Black Resistance and the Struggle for a New South Africa*. Boston: Beacon Press, 1990.

Mulholland, Rosemary. *South Africa, 1948–1994*. New York: Cambridge University Press, 1997.

Nuttall, Michael. *Number Two to Tutu: A Memoir*. Pietermaritzburg: Cluster Publications, 2003.

Paris, Erna. *Long Shadows: Truth, Lies and History.* New York: Bloomsbury, 2001.
Paton, Alan. *Apartheid and the Archbishop: The Life and Times of Geoffrey Clayton.* New York: Charles Scribner's Sons, 1973.
Sparks, Allister. *Beyond the Miracle: Inside the New South Africa.* Chicago: University of Chicago Press, 2003.
Tlhagale, Buti, and Itumeleng Mosala, eds. *Hammering Swords into Ploughshares: Essays in Honor of Archbishop Mpilo Desmond Tutu.* Grand Rapids, MI: William B. Eerdmans, 1987.
Winner, David. *Desmond Tutu.* People Who Helped the World Series. Harrisburg, PA: Morehouse, 1989.

PERIODICALS

Archbishop Desmond Tutu to P.W. Botha. *Ecunews* 14 (8 April 1988): pp. 14–16.
"Archbishop Tutu's Message to America." *Sunday Independent,* 4 November 2001.
"Bishop Tutu Presses Case for Freedom as Tension in South Africa Continues." *Wall Street Journal,* 16 June 1986.
"Bishop Tutu Sees a 'Catastrophe' for South Africa." *New York Times,* 17 August 1985.
"Bishop Tutu's Hopes and Fears." *Time,* 19 August 1985.
Davies, Geoffrey. "Tutu—The Man I Know." *Ecunews* 8 (December 1984): pp. 14–15.
"Desmond Tutu: 'There's life after prostate cancer.'" *Ebony,* February 1998, pp. 166–68.
Hope, Marjorie, and James Young. "Desmond Mpilo Tutu: South Africa's Doughty Black Bishop." *Christian Century* 97, no. 43 (31 December 1980): pp. 1290–94.
"It's Wonderful to Be Alive at a Moment Like This." *Minneapolis Star Tribune,* 26 February 2003.
Lelyveld, Joseph. "South Africa's Bishop Tutu." *New York Times Magazine,* 14 March 1982, pp. 22–25, 40, 42, 44, 102–3, 106–7.
Matthews, Christopher. "The Prayers of Desmond Tutu." *San Francisco Examiner,* 1 May 1994.
Mutloatse, Mothobi. "Mutloatse on Tutu." *Ecunews* 8 (December 1984): pp. 15–17.
Paton, Alan. "Paton on Tutu." *Sunday Times,* 21 October 1984.
"Reflections on War, Peace, and How to Live Vitally and Act Globally." *New York Times,* 1 June 2003.
"S. African Report Draws Bitterness." *Washington Post,* 30 October 1998.

Schleier, Curt. "Desmond Mpilo Tutu." *Investor's Business Daily*, 3 April 2001.

"Searching for New Worlds." *Time*, 29 October 1984.

Serfontein, J. H. P. "Tutu—The Man of Peace." *Ecunews* 8 (December 1984): pp. 18–19.

"South African Commission Ends Its Work." *New York Times*, 22 March 2003.

"South Africa Snubs Tutu, May Oust Foreign Workers." *Chicago Tribune*, 30 July 1985.

"Tutu: America Led Way for His Nation." *Birmingham News*, 19 April 2002.

"Tutu Asks U.S. Jews to Urge Palestinian Pact." *New York Times*, 4 February 1989.

"Tutu Praises U.S. Public's Role in Forcing Action Against Apartheid." *Los Angeles Times*, 21 January 1986.

"Tutu Rakes U.S. Policy on S. Africa." *Quad City Times*, 26 May 1987.

"Tutu Urges Barring South Africa from the Olympics in Barcelona." *New York Times*, 23 June 1992.

"We Can Overcome Our Problems: Tutu." *ANC Daily News Briefing*, 9 October 2001.

INTERNET SOURCES

Desmond Tutu Peace Centre home page. www.tutu.org.

Hall of Public Service. Interview with Archbishop Desmond Tutu, Washington, D.C., 2 May 2003. www.achievement.org/autodoc/page/tut0int-1.

Jacksonville.com. "Tutu Calls on Bush to Work with UN on Iraq." 8 January 2003. www.jacksonville.com/tu-online/stories/010803/met_11414418.shtml.

Truth and Reconciliation Commission home page. www.doj.gov.za/trc/.

University of Minnesota–Twin Cities. "Great Conversations—Desmond Tutu." 25 February 2003. www.news.mpr.org/programs/midday/listings/md 20030303.shtml.

VIDEOTAPE

Archbishop Desmond Tutu with Bill Moyers. VHS. Princeton, NJ: Films for the Humanities and Sciences, 1999.

INTERVIEW

Desmond Tutu, in discussion with the author. 29 April 2003, Jacksonville, FL.

INDEX

About the Author

STEVEN D. GISH is Associate Professor of History at Auburn University of Montgomery in Alabama and specializes in the South African and African history.